Next-Generation ACCUPLACER Exam Practice Questions

ACCUPLACER Practice Tests & Review for the Next-Generation ACCUPLACER Exam

D1595074

Dear Future Exam Success Story:

First of all, **THANK YOU** for purchasing Mometrix study materials!

Second, congratulations! You are one of the few determined test-takers who are committed to doing whatever it takes to excel on your exam. **You have come to the right place.** We developed these practice tests with one goal in mind: to deliver you the best possible approximation of the questions you will see on test day.

Standardized testing is one of the biggest obstacles on your road to success, which only increases the importance of doing well in the high-pressure, high-stakes environment of test day. Your results on this test could have a significant impact on your future, and these practice tests will give you the repetitions you need to build your familiarity and confidence with the test content and format to help you achieve your full potential on test day.

Your success is our success

We would love to hear from you! If you would like to share the story of your exam success or if you have any questions or comments in regard to our products, please contact us at **800-673-8175** or **support@mometrix.com**.

Thanks again for your business and we wish you continued success!

Sincerely,
The Mometrix Test Preparation Team

TABLE OF CONTENTS

PRACTICE TEST #1 ....**1**

    READING.. 1

    WRITING... 8

    MATHEMATICS 14

ANSWER EXPLANATIONS #1...**26**

    READING.. 26

    WRITING... 28

    MATHEMATICS 30

PRACTICE TEST #2 ....**41**

    READING.. 41

    WRITING... 49

    MATHEMATICS 56

ANSWER EXPLANATIONS #2...**69**

    READING.. 69

    WRITING... 70

    MATHEMATICS 73

THANK YOU...**84**

Practice Test #1

Reading

It is a truth universally acknowledged, that a single man in possession of a good fortune, must be in want of a wife.

However little known the feelings or views of such a man may be on his first entering a neighbourhood, this truth is so well fixed in the minds of the surrounding families, that he is considered the rightful property of some one or other of their daughters.

"My dear Mr. Bennet," said his lady to him one day, "have you heard that Netherfield Park is let at last?"

Mr. Bennet replied that he had not.

"But it is," returned she; "for Mrs. Long has just been here, and she told me all about it."

Mr. Bennet made no answer.

"Do you not want to know who has taken it?" cried his wife impatiently.

"You want to tell me, and I have no objection to hearing it."

This was invitation enough.

"Why, my dear, you must know, Mrs. Long says that Netherfield is taken by a young man of large fortune from the north of England; that he came down on Monday in a chaise and four to see the place, and was so much delighted with it, that he agreed with Mr. Morris immediately; that he is to take possession before Michaelmas, and some of his servants are to be in the house by the end of next week."

"What is his name?"

"Bingley."

"Is he married or single?"

"Oh! Single, my dear, to be sure! A single man of large fortune; four or five thousand a year. What a fine thing for our girls!"

"How so? How can it affect them?"

"My dear Mr. Bennet," replied his wife, "how can you be so tiresome! You must know that I am thinking of his marrying one of them."

"Is that his design in settling here?"

"Design! Nonsense, how can you talk so! But it is very likely that he may fall in love with one of them, and therefore you must visit him as soon as he comes."

- 1 -

"I see no occasion for that. You and the girls may go, or you may send them by themselves, which perhaps will be still better, for as you are as handsome as any of them, Mr. Bingley may like you the best of the party."

[Adapted from Jane Austen, *Pride and Prejudice* (1813)]

1. What is the central idea of this selection?
   a. A new neighbor is due to arrive who may become good friends with Mr. and Mrs. Bennet.
   b. A new neighbor is due to arrive who may be a prospective husband for one of the Bennet daughters.
   c. A new neighbor is due to arrive who may be a good business connection for Mr. Bennet.
   d. A new neighbor is due to arrive who has already expressed an interest in marrying one of the Bennet daughters.

2. Which of the following statements best describes Mrs. Bennet's feelings about her husband as indicated by this selection?
   a. Mrs. Bennet is tired of her husband.
   b. Mrs. Bennet is exasperated by her husband.
   c. Mrs. Bennet is afraid of her husband.
   d. Mrs. Bennet is indifferent toward her husband.

3. This selection is set in England at the beginning of the 19th century. Drawing on information from this selection, what could you conclude was a primary goal for young women in England during this time period?
   a. To marry
   b. To marry a man with money
   c. To entertain the neighbors
   d. To be courted by as many men as possible

4. "Is that his design in settling here?"

What does the word design mean in the context of this selection?
   a. Intention
   b. Drawing
   c. Creation
   d. Improvisation

Passage One

Black History Month is unnecessary. In a place and time in which we overwhelmingly elected an African American president, we can and should move to a post-racial approach to education. As *Detroit Free Press* columnist Rochelle Riley wrote in a February 1 column calling for an end to Black History Month, "I propose that, for the first time in American history, this country has reached a point where we can stop celebrating separately, stop learning separately, stop being American separately."

In addition to being unnecessary, the idea that African American history should be focused on in a given month suggests that it belongs in that month alone. It is important to instead incorporate African American history into what is taught every day as American history. It needs to be recreated as part of mainstream thought and not as an optional, often irrelevant, side note. We should focus efforts on pushing schools to diversify and broaden their curricula.

- 2 -

There are a number of other reasons to abolish it: first, it has become a shallow commercial ritual that does not even succeed in its (limited and misguided) goal of focusing for one month on a sophisticated, intelligent appraisal of the contributions and experiences of African Americans throughout history. Second, there is a paternalistic flavor to the mandated bestowing of a month in which to study African American history that is overcome if we instead assert the need for a comprehensive curriculum. Third, the idea of Black History Month suggests that the knowledge imparted in that month is for African Americans only, rather than for all people.

Passage Two

Black History Month is still an important observance. Despite the important achievement of the election of our first African American president, the need for knowledge and education about African American history is still unmet to a substantial degree. Black History Month is a powerful tool in working towards meeting that need. There is no reason to give up that tool now, and it can easily coexist with an effort to develop a more comprehensive and inclusive yearly curriculum.

Having a month set aside for the study of African American history doesn't limit its study and celebration to that month; it merely focuses complete attention on it for that month. There is absolutely no contradiction between having a set-aside month and having it be present in the curriculum the rest of the year.

Equally important is that the debate *itself* about the usefulness of Black History Month can, and should, remind parents that they can't necessarily count on schools to teach African American history as thoroughly as many parents would want.

Although Black History Month has, to an extent, become a shallow ritual, it doesn't have to be. Good teachers and good materials could make the February curriculum deeply informative, thought-provoking, and inspiring. The range of material that can be covered is rich, varied, and full of limitless possibilities.

Finally, it is worthwhile to remind ourselves and our children of the key events that happened during the month of February. In 1926, Woodson organized the first Black History Week to honor the birthdays of essential civil rights activists Abraham Lincoln and Frederick Douglass. W. E. B. DuBois was born on February 23, 1868. The 15th Amendment, which granted African Americans the right to vote, was passed on February 3, 1870. The first black U.S. senator, Hiram R. Revels, took his oath of office on February 25, 1870. The National Association for the Advancement of Colored People (NAACP) was founded on February 12, 1909. Malcolm X was shot on February 21, 1965.

5. The author's primary purpose in Passage 1 is to:
    a. argue that Black History Month should not be so commercial.
    b. argue that Black History Month should be abolished.
    c. argue that Black History Month should be maintained.
    d. suggest that African American history should be taught in two months rather than just one.

6. It can be inferred that the term "post-racial" in the second sentence of Passage 1 refers to an approach that:
    a. treats race as the most important factor in determining an individual's experience.
    b. treats race as one factor, but not the most important, in determining an individual's experience.
    c. considers race after considering all other elements of a person's identity.
    d. is not based on or organized around concepts of race.

7. Which of the following statements is true?
    a. The author of Passage 1 thinks that it is important for students to learn about the achievements and experience of African Americans, while the author of Passage 2 does not think this is important.
    b. The author of Passage 2 thinks that it is important for students to learn about the achievements and experience of African Americans, while the author of Passage 1 does not think this is important.
    c. Neither author thinks that it is important for students to learn about the achievements and experience of African Americans.
    d. Both authors think that it is important for students to learn about the achievements and experience of African Americans.

8. The author of Passage 1 argues that celebrating Black History Month suggests that the study of African American history can and should be limited to one month of the year. What is the author of Passage 2's response?
    a. Black History Month is still an important observance.
    b. Black History Month is a powerful tool in meeting the need for education about African American history.
    c. Having a month set aside for the study of African American history does not limit its study and celebration to that month.
    d. Black History Month does not have to be a shallow ritual.

It is believed that the diamond was originally discovered and extracted in India as much as 6,000 years ago. The word *diamond*, however, derives from the Greek αδαμας, or *adámas*, which means "unbreakable" or even "untamed," and has made its way into Western literature through the Greek tradition. Having heard rumors of exceptionally strong stones, the Greeks developed a mythology about an unbreakable stone that was known as *adamant*. By the Middle Ages, this came to be recognized as the diamond. Over time, the legendary adamant came to take on a mystical quality that passed into certain forms of medieval literature and even today has an allegorical place in some genres.

9. The statements made in the passage above support which of the following claims?
    a. Given the legendary status of the adamant, it might have been better if the diamond and its actual qualities had remained a mystery.
    b. Because the adamant was originally associated with mythical qualities, it retains figurative attributes that are still valuable for some writers.
    c. The diamond and the adamant are essentially the same gem, and the two terms can be interchanged.
    d. The Greek word *adámas* is based on an ancient word of India that meant the same thing but has now been lost to history.

Colorblindness is a vision deficiency that limits the ability of the sufferer to see certain colors clearly. The condition may affect a person in varying degrees, ranging from mild colorblindness with a red or green color deficiency to complete colorblindness with no ability to distinguish any colors beside dim shades of brown. The primary cause of colorblindness is believed to be a mutation on the X chromosome. Men carry a single X chromosome, possessing an XY-chromosome makeup, while women carry two X chromosomes, thus having the potential to combat colorblindness with an extra X chromosome.

10. If the passage above is true, which of the following can be inferred from it?
   a. Colorblindness is a rare condition that affects very few members of the population.
   b. Despite the handicap, those who are colorblind might have certain advantages, particularly in seeing camouflage.
   c. Women alone are capable of passing on a gene for colorblindness.
   d. Because of the way colorblindness affects the X chromosome, men are more likely to be colorblind than women.

Some of our most delighted *voyageurs* are from Portland, Maine. When they had journeyed some 1,500 miles to Omaha they imagined themselves at least half way across our continent. Then, when they had finished that magnificent stretch of some 1,700 miles more from Omaha to Portland, Oregon, in the palace cars of the Union Pacific, they were quite sure of it. Of course, they confessed a sense of mingled disappointment and eager anticipation when they learned that they were yet less than half way. They learned what is a fact—that the extreme west coast of Alaska is as far west of Sitka as Portland, Maine, is east of Portland, Oregon, and the further fact that San Francisco lacks 4,000 miles of being as far west as Uncle Sam's "Land's End," at extreme Western Alaska.

11. What is the main purpose of the paragraph?
   a. To convey the awe and delight the group felt at seeing the sights of Alaska
   b. To describe the people in the group
   c. To show the great distance and size of Alaska
   d. To explain that San Francisco lacks 4,000 miles of being as far west as Uncle Sam's "Land's End"

Psychologists have found that there are fascinating differences between children and adults when it comes to learning a new musical instrument. In particular, the piano is an instrument that knows no one age for learning and presents multiple opportunities for the successful attainment of musical skills. It does, however, offer a variety of challenges both to children and to adults – due to the differences in mind development – with children developing certain skills more quickly and more effectively than adults. How quickly children learn is often limited by their motor skills, but they are more likely to remember in detail the pieces they learn and to retain that knowledge over long periods of time. At the same time, adults are more likely to retain the muscle memory of the pieces that they learn and reproduce them blindly, just by allowing their fingers to recall the correct notes.

12. If the passage above is true, all of the following may be concluded EXCEPT:
   a. Adult minds learn the skills required to play the piano differently than children's minds.
   b. Adults might not recall the exact details of the piece they learned, but the muscle memory in their fingers makes them very likely to remember the notes.
   c. The piano is the only instrument that both children and adults can learn to play well.
   d. Learning the piano is not limited to children, because adults can learn to play well.

The climate extremes of the North Atlantic nation of Iceland ensure that little plant growth will be able to survive there. The majority of the island is covered in low grasses, with only one tree species known to exist. Deforestation in previous centuries depopulated the entire island of its trees. Because of both the severe cold and the severe heat, plants require a long period of time to grow in Iceland, and modern residents have only just begun replanting the trees. Plant life in

- 5 -

Iceland is also notoriously delicate, and off-road vehicles are allowed only in certain areas; in some cases, hikers are required to walk around certain plants to ensure that the plants will survive even during the extreme weather that constantly surrounds Iceland.

13. Considering the claims below within the context of the passage above, which claim is most likely to be true?
>   a. More developed plant growth exists closer to the island's center, where volcanic warmth allows the plants to survive.
>   b. The plants that manage to survive in Iceland are extremely hardy.
>   c. The only type of tree capable of growing successfully in Iceland is the northern birch.
>   d. Off-road vehicles can cause permanent or long-term damage to the re-growth of some plants.

A local farmer is hoping to establish a certified organic farm but is concerned about the cost of setting it up. A certified organic farm requires far fewer supplies than a non-organic farm, and most of the supplies are less costly in comparison. Also, because an organic farm does not use expensive pesticides or tools, the cost of maintenance is also fairly low in comparison to the maintenance cost of a non-organic farm. But the set-up of the certified organic farm remains expensive, and the farmer is unsure if the return on his investment will justify the cost.

14. Which of the following statements best explains the farmer's concern about the high cost of setting up a certified organic farm?
>   a. There is little demand in the community for more certified organic food.
>   b. More resources are required for establishing a certified organic farm than a non-organic farm.
>   c. There are three other certified organic farms in the community that are much larger than the farm the farmer is planning to establish.
>   d. The licensing fees for the farmer to acquire certification add considerably to the cost of set-up.

Are video games without pitfalls? Certainly not. But many games offer life-improving benefits that are often overlooked. They improve coordination and response time. They enhance logic and reasoning. They fill empty hours productively and create a sense of passion and excitement. Lastly, video games foster a variety of social bonds among players of all types, skill levels, and backgrounds. With so many positive aspects, video games are worth checking out. Try them—you might find you like them!

15. Which of the following best summarizes the paragraph above?
>   a. Video games are good for everyone
>   b. Video games have a number of pitfalls
>   c. Social bonds are one of the greatest benefits of video games
>   d. Despite the pitfalls, video games are worth trying

It is supposed that the Phoenicians, who were an ancient people, famous for carrying on trade, came in ships to these Islands, and found that they produced tin and lead; both very useful things, as you know, and both produced to this very hour upon the sea-coast. The most celebrated tin mines in Cornwall are, still, close to the sea. One of them, which I have seen, is so close to it that it is hollowed out underneath the ocean; and the miners say, that in stormy weather, when they are at work down in that deep place, they can hear the noise of the waves thundering above their heads.

So, the Phoenicians, coasting about the Islands, would come, without much difficulty, to where the tin and lead were.

16. The tone of this passage is
    a. humorous
    b. informative
    c. angry
    d. bored

Many of the concepts utilized in crew resource management (CRM) have been successfully applied to single-pilot operations which led to the development of single-pilot resource management (SRM). Defined as the art and science of managing all the resources (both on board the aircraft and from outside resources) available to a single pilot (prior to and during flight), SRM ensures the successful outcome of the flight. SRM training helps the pilot maintain situational awareness by managing automation, associated control, and navigation tasks. This enables the pilot to accurately assess hazards, manage resulting risk potential, and make good decisions. To make informed decisions during flight operations, a pilot must be aware of the resources found both inside and outside the cockpit. Resources must not only be identified, but a pilot must also develop the skills to evaluate whether he or she has the time to use a particular resource and the impact its use has upon the safety of flight.

17. What is the author's purpose in writing this passage?
    a. To describe single-pilot resource management
    b. To compare single-pilot resource management to crew resource management
    c. To persuade readers to use single-pilot resource management
    d. To answer objections to single-pilot resource management

18. Since Glenda was short of money, she decided that her current appliances were _____ for the present.
    a. ephemeral
    b. imperious
    c. pestilent
    d. sufficient

19. The varsity basketball team's perfect season _____ in a championship win over their biggest rival.
    a. alleviated
    b. culminated
    c. dispersed
    d. lamented

20. The forecaster said that the high winds would _____ about midnight and that the next day would have light breezes.
    a. capitulate
    b. dispatch
    c. intensify
    d. subside

Writing

(1) My favorite song is "imagine" by John Lennon. (2) It was released in 1971. (3) It is one of the few famous songs that John Lennon recorded and sang alone. (4) For the majority of his career, John Lennon was a member of an iconic rock band called the Beatles, a band that changed the music industry. (5) The Beatles accepted a lot of success in their career, with popular songs such as "I Want to Hold Your Hand," "Come Together," "Let it Be," and "Here Comes the Sun." (6) After the band decided to separate, John Lennon became a solo artist as well as a promoter for peace.

(7) "Imagine" tells the story of Lennons dream of peace in the world. He asks the listener to imagine different situations. (8) He says to imagine that there are no countries, religions, or possessions. (9) He says, "I wonder if you can." (10) This line strikes me the most I try to imagine such a world. (11) When talking about no possessions, he continues and says, "No need for greed or hunger." (12) It is a great line. (13) Throughout the song, he says, "Imagine all the people." (14) And he gives examples. (15) At first he says, "living for today," and then moves on to say, "living life in peace," and finally, "sharing all the world."

(16) My favorite part of the song is the chorus. (17) Lennon says, "You may say I'm a dreamer, but I'm not the only one. (18) I hope someday you'll join us, and the world will be as one." (19) When I really listen to the words of this song, I realize that "Imagine" is so much more than something that sounds nicely. (20) Lennon is saying something very important and suggesting ways in which the world can live in peace. (21) Because of this song, I am a dreamer as well, and I join John Lennon in the fight for world peace.

1. What is the BEST way to revise sentence 2?
   a. Although it was released in 1971, the lyrics are still important today.
   b. The song is just as popular today as it was in 1971.
   c. The song was released in 1971.
   d. No revision needed.

2. What is the BEST verb to replace *accepted* in sentence 5?
   a. Lasted
   b. Liked
   c. Had
   d. Watched

3. What is the BEST way to revise sentence 10?
   a. This line strikes me the most as I try to imagine such a world.
   b. This line strikes me the most, I try to imagine such a world.
   c. This line strikes me, the most. I try to imagine such a world.
   d. No revision needed.

4. What is the BEST way to combine sentence 13 and sentence 14?
   a. Throughout the song he says "Imagine all the people" and he gives examples.
   b. Throughout the song, he says, "Imagine all the people," and he gives examples.
   c. Throughout the song he says Imagine all the people, and he gives examples.
   d. Throughout the song he says Imagine all the people and he gives examples.

5. What change should be made in sentence 19?

    a. Delete the comma after *song*
    b. Change *something* to *some thing*
    c. Change *nicely* to *nice*
    d. Change *realize* to *realized*

(1) In Ruth Campbell's book Exploring the Titanic, the events of the famous ship's only journey and sinking are brought to life. (2) In 1912, Titanic was built and was the largest passenger steamship at the time. (3) On what would be its first and only journey, the ship departed from Southampton in England and was supposed to arrive in New York City. (4) The ship hit an iceberg late at night on April 14, 1912, and sunked less than three hours later.

(5) Titanic was designed by some of the best engineers and had the latest technology of the time. (6) The ship was made to carry over three and a half thousand passengers and crew members, but had only twenty lifeboats. (7) There was not enough lifeboats for all of the people onboard, and as a result, only seven hundred six people survived.

(8) One interesting thing about Titanic, is that the ship was divided into classes. (9) The most expensive tickets were first class, and first class passengers had the biggest and much luxurious rooms. (10) The first class rooms were the closest to the ship's deck. (11) Because this the majority of survivors came from first class. (12) They were able to reach the deck fastest to get a seat on a lifeboat. (13) The third class rooms were located the farthest below deck, and the majority of the third class passengers did not survive.

(14) Ruth Campbell's book was very interesting but also sad because the story of Titanic is true. (15) However, Campbell ended the book by talking about the positive things that have happened because of this tragedy. (16) Most importantly, experts now recommend that ships' carry enough lifeboats for all passengers onboard. (17) This would have saved a lot of lifes. (18) It was a good book, and it displayed a good message in history that lessons should be learned from mistakes.

6. What change should be made in sentence 1?

    a. Change ship's to ships
    b. Insert a comma after book
    c. Change are to is
    d. Change brought to bring

7. What change should be made in sentence 7?

    a. Change There to They're
    b. Delete the comma after onboard
    c. Change lifeboats to lifeboats'
    d. Change was to were

8. What change, if any, should be made in sentence 8?

    a. Change was to were
    b. Delete the comma after Titanic
    c. Change divided into divide
    d. Make no change

9. What is the BEST way to revise and combine sentence 11 and sentence 12?

   a. Because, the majority of survivors came from first class as they were able to reach the deck fastest to get a seat on a lifeboat
   b. Because of this, the majority of survivors came from first class, as they were able to reach the deck fastest to get a seat on a lifeboat
   c. Because this, the majority of survivors came from first class, they were able to reach the deck fastest to get a seat on a lifeboat
   d. Because of this, the majority of survivors came from first class as they were able to reach the deck fastest to get a seat on a lifeboat

10. What is the BEST transition word that could be added to the beginning of sentence 13?

   a. Lastly
   b. However
   c. Additionally
   d. Therefore

(1) Basketball is, arguably, one of the most popular and most exciting sports of our time. (2) Behind this fast-paced sport, however, is a rich history. (3) There have been many changes made to the game over the years, but the essence remains the same. (4) From it's humble beginnings in 1891, basketball has grown to have worldwide appeal.

(5) One thing that sets the history of basketball apart from other major sports is the fact that it was created by just one man. (6) In 1891, Dr. James Naismith, a teacher and Presbyterian Minister, needed an indoor game to keep college students at the Springfield, Massachusetts YMCA Training School busy during long winter days. (7) This need prompted the creation of basketball, which was originally played by tossing a soccer ball into an empty peach basket nailed to the gym wall. (8) There was two teams, but only one basket in the original game.

(9) Because of the simplicity of basketball, the game had spread across the nation within 30 years of its invention in Massachusetts. (10) As more teams formed, the need for a league became apparent. (11) The smaller National Basketball League (NBL) formed soon after. (12) On June 6, 1946, the Basketball Association of America (BAA) was formed. (13) In 1948, the BAA absconded the NBL, and the National Basketball Association (NBA) was born. (14) The NBA played its first full season in 1948-49 and is still going strong today.

(15) Though much has changed in our world since 1891, the popularity of the sport of basketball has remained strong. (16) From it's humble start in a YMCA gym to the multi-million-dollar empire it is today, the simple fun of the sport has endured. (17) Although many changes have been made over the years, the essence of basketball has remained constant. (18) Its rich history and simplicity ensure that basketball will always be a popular sport around the world.

11. What is the BEST way to revise and combine sentence 2 and sentence 3?

   a. Behind this fast-paced sport is a rich history; however, there have been many changes made to the game over the years.
   b. Over the years the essence remains the same for this fast-paced sport with its rich history.
   c. Behind this fast-paced sport is a rich history, but the essence remains the same.
   d. There have been many changes made to this fast-paced sport over the years, but the essence remains the same due to its rich history.

12. How would you correct sentence 4 in this essay?
   a. Change beginnings to beginning
   b. Change worldwide to world-wide
   c. Change has to had
   d. Change it's to its

13. What correction, if any, is necessary in sentence 8?
   a. No correction is necessary
   b. Change was to were
   c. Write the numbers as numerals instead of words
   d. Remove the comma

14. Which of the following changes would most improve the organization and clarity of paragraph 3 of this essay?
   a. The paragraph is correct as it is written
   b. Move sentence 10 to the beginning of the paragraph
   c. Switch sentences 11 and 12
   d. Switch sentences 13 and 14

15. What change, if any, is needed in sentence 16?
   a. No change is needed
   b. Change it's to its
   c. Remove the hyphens from multi-million-dollar
   d. Remove the comma after today

(1) Most scientists agree that while the scientific method is an invaluable methodological tool, it is not a failsafe method for arriving at objective truth. (2) It is debatable, for example, whether a hypothesis can actually be confirmed by evidence.

(3) When the hypothesis is of a form, "All x are y," which is commonly believed that a piece of evidence that is both x and y confirms the hypothesis. (4) For example, for the hypothesis "All monkeys are hairy," a particular monkey that is hairy is thought to be a confirming piece of evidence for the hypothesis. (5) A problem arises when one encounters evidence that disproves a hypothesis: while no scientist would argue that one piece of evidence proves a hypothesis, it is possible for one piece of evidence to disprove a hypothesis. (6) To return to the monkey example, one hairless monkey out of one billion hairy monkeys disproves the hypothesis "All monkeys are hairy." (7) Single pieces of evidence, then, seem to affect a given hypothesis in radically different ways. (8) For this reason, the confirmation of hypotheses is better described as probabilistic.

(9) Hypotheses that can only be proven or disproven based on evidence need to be based on probability because sample sets for such hypotheses are too large. (10) In the monkey example, every single monkey in the history of monkeys would need to be examined before the hypothesis could be proven. (11) By making confirmation a function of probability, one may make provisional or working conclusions that allow for the possibility of a given hypothesis being dissipated in the future. (12) In the monkey case, then, encountering a hairy monkey would slightly raise the probability that "all monkeys are hairy," while encountering a hairless monkey would slightly decrease the probability that "all monkeys are hairy." (13) This method of confirming hypotheses is both counterintuitive and controversial, but it allowed for evidence to equitably effect hypotheses and it does not require infinite sample sets for confirmation or disconfirmation.

16. Which is the best placement for sentence 4 in this passage?

    a. Before sentence 3
    b. After sentence 6
    c. After sentence 7
    d. In its current place

17. Which choice most effectively transitions from sentence 7 to sentence 8 (reproduced below) at the underlined portion?

Single pieces of evidence, then, seem to affect a given hypothesis in radically <u>different ways. For this reason, the confirmation</u> of hypotheses is better described as probabilistic.

    a. different ways, but the confirmation
    b. different ways; therefore, the confirmation
    c. different ways--the confirmation
    d. different ways; however, for this reason, the confirmation

18. What is the best change to make for sentence 11?

    a. No Change
    b. distilled
    c. disconfirmed
    d. destroyed

19. What is the best change for sentence 13?

    a. No Change
    b. but it allows for evidence to equitably effect hypotheses
    c. but it allowed for evidence to equitably affect hypotheses
    d. but it allows for evidence to equitably affect hypotheses

20. This passage ends with, "...it does not require infinite sample sets for confirmation or disconfirmation." This statement refers to information found where in the passage?

    a. Most specifically in the initial sentence in this same paragraph
    b. Most specifically in the second sentence of the same paragraph
    c. Most specifically the fourth sentence of the previous paragraph
    d. Most specifically the information is not found in any paragraph

(1) The islands of New Zealand are among the most remote of all the Pacific islands. (2) New Zealand is an archipelago, with two large islands and a number of smaller ones. (3) Its climate is far cooler than the rest of Polynesia. (4) According to Maori legends, it was colonized in the early fifteenth century by a wave of Polynesian voyagers who traveled southward in their canoes and settled on North Island. (5) At this time, New Zealand will already be known to the Polynesians, who had probably first landed there some 400 years earlier.

(6) The Polynesian southward migration was limited by the availability of food. (7) Traditional Polynesian tropical crops such as taro and yams will grow on North Island, but the climate of South Island is too cold for them. (8) Coconuts will not grow on either island. (9) The first settlers were forced to rely on hunting and gathering, and, of course, fishing. (10) Especially on South Island, most settlements remained close to the sea. (11) At the time of the Polynesian incursion, enormous flocks of moa birds had their rookeries on the island shores. (12) These flightless birds were easy prey for the settlers, and within a few centuries had been hunted to extinction. (13) Fish, shellfish and the roots of the fern were other important sources of food, but even these began to diminish in

quantity as the human population increased. (14) The Maori had few other sources of meat: dogs, smaller birds, and rats. (15) Archaeological evidence shows that human flesh was also eaten, and that tribal warfare increased markedly after the moa disappeared.

(16) By far the most important farmed crop in prehistoric New Zealand was the sweet potato. (17) This tuber is hearty enough to grow throughout the islands, and could be stored to provide food during the winter months, when other food-gathering activities were difficult. (18) The availability of the sweet potato made possible a significant increase in the human population. (19) Maori tribes often lived in encampments called *pa*, which were fortified with earthen embankments and usually located near the best sweet potato farmlands.

21. What is the BEST way to revise and combine sentence 2 and sentence 3?
    a. Its climate is far cooler than the rest of Polynesia because New Zealand is an archipelago, with two large islands and a number of smaller ones.
    b. New Zealand is an archipelago, with two large islands and a number of smaller ones, and its climate is far cooler than the rest of Polynesia.
    c. Its climate is far cooler than the rest of Polynesia; however, New Zealand is an archipelago, with two large islands and a number of smaller ones.
    d. New Zealand is an archipelago, with two large islands and a number of smaller ones; thus, its climate is far cooler than the rest of Polynesia.

22. What is the best change for sentence 5?
    a. No Change
    b. New Zealand is already known by the Polynesians
    c. New Zealand has already been known to the Polynesians
    d. New Zealand was already known to the Polynesians

23. What is the best change to make for sentence 11?
    a. No Change
    b. import
    c. influx
    d. gathering

24. Which choice most effectively transitions from sentence 9 to sentence 10 (reproduced below) at the underlined portion?
The first settlers were forced to rely on hunting and gathering, and, of course, fishing. Especially on South Island, most settlements remained close to the sea.

    a. of course, fishing, but especially on South Island
    b. of course, fishing; however, on South Island
    c. of course, fishing: especially on South Island
    d. of course, fishing; therefore, on South Island

25. Which is the best placement for sentence 18 in this passage?
    a. Before sentence 16
    b. After sentence 16
    c. After sentence 19
    d. In its current place

Mathematics

Arithmetic

Solve the following problems and select your answer from the choices given. You may use the paper you have been given for scratch paper.

1. Which of the following is equivalent to $\frac{27}{8}$?

    a. $2\frac{7}{8}$
    b. $3\frac{3}{8}$
    c. $4\frac{5}{8}$
    d. $9\frac{3}{8}$

2. $6.32 - 3.5 =$

    a. 2.82
    b. 3.18
    c. 3.27
    d. 5.97

3. A box is 30 cm long, 20 cm wide, and 15 cm high. What is the volume of the box?

    a. 65 cm^3
    b. 260 cm^3
    c. $1,125 \text{ cm}^3$
    d. $9,000 \text{ cm}^3$

4. What is the proper ordering (from greatest to least) of the following numbers?

    I. 0.071%
    II. 0.71
    III. 7.1%
    IV. $\frac{71}{101}$

    a. II, III, I, IV
    b. II, IV, III, I
    c. III, II, I, IV
    d. IV, I, III, II

5. 9.5% of the people in a town voted for a certain proposition in a municipal election. If the town's population is 51,623, about how many people in the town voted for the proposition?

    a. 3,000
    b. 5,000
    c. 7,000
    d. 10,000

6. What is $\frac{5}{6}$ of $\frac{3}{4}$?

    a. $\frac{2}{3}$

    b. $\frac{3}{5}$

    c. $\frac{4}{5}$

    d. $\frac{5}{8}$

7. There are twelve inches in a foot, and three feet in a yard. How many inches are in five yards?

    a. 20

    b. 41

    c. 75

    d. 180

8. $2.2 \times 31.3 =$

    a. 6.886

    b. 68.86

    c. 688.6

    d. 6886.00

9. What is the average of $\frac{1}{3}$, $\frac{2}{3}$, and $\frac{1}{4}$?

    a. $\frac{1}{2}$

    b. $\frac{2}{5}$

    c. $\frac{3}{8}$

    d. $\frac{5}{12}$

10. Which of the following inequalities is TRUE?

    a. $\frac{7}{8} < \frac{6}{7}$

    b. $\frac{9}{10} > \frac{11}{12}$

    c. $\frac{2}{3} > \frac{9}{13}$

    d. $\frac{1}{4} < \frac{2}{7}$

11. Which of the following is equal to 0.0023?

    a. 2.3×10^{-3}

    b. 2.3×10^{-2}

    c. 2.3×10^{2}

    d. 2.3×10^{3}

12. A reporter for a school newspaper surveys the students at the school to ask if they prefer chocolate, vanilla, or strawberry ice cream. Of the students who answer her question, 35% prefer vanilla, and 40% prefer chocolate. What percent of the students she surveyed prefer strawberry?

    a. 15%

    b. 25%

    c. 45%

    d. There is not enough information to say.

13. A cookie recipe calls for $2\frac{1}{4}$ cups of milk. Brian has $1\frac{1}{2}$ cups available. How much more milk does he need in order to make cookies according to the recipe?

    a. $1\frac{1}{2}$ cups

    b. $1\frac{1}{4}$ cups

    c. $\frac{3}{4}$ cup

    d. $\frac{1}{4}$ cup

14. Which of the following fractions is closest to $\frac{15,012}{19,938}$?

    a. $\frac{1}{4}$

    b. $\frac{3}{4}$

    c. $\frac{4}{5}$

    d. $\frac{5}{9}$

15. $\frac{2}{5} \times 2.5 =$

    a. 1
    b. 2
    c. 4
    d. 6

16. Which of the following represents the largest number?

    a. $\left(\frac{1}{3}\right)^{-4}$

    b. $9^{\frac{3}{2}}$

    c. $27^{\frac{2}{3}}$

    d. $3^{-\frac{25}{3}}$

17. Sam runs for fifteen minutes at eight miles per hour, and then jogs for forty-five minutes at four miles per hour. What is his average speed during this time?

    a. 5 miles per hour
    b. 5.5 miles per hour
    c. 6 miles per hour
    d. 7 miles per hour

18. In the diagram to the right, all five angles are equal. What is the measure of each angle?

    a. 20°
    b. 36°
    c. 60°
    d. 72°

19. What percent of 800 is 40?

    a. 2%

    b. 5%

    c. 20%

    d. 32%

20. $\frac{3}{16} =$

    a. 0.025

    b. 0.533

    c. 0.1875

    d. 0.2025

Quantitative Reasoning, Algebra, and Statistics

Solve the following problems and select your answer from the choices given. You may use the paper you have been given for scratch paper.

21. Which of the following is equivalent to $3 - 2x < 5$?

    a. $x < 1$

    b. $x > 1$

    c. $x < -1$

    d. $x > -1$

22. $6\left(-\frac{2}{3}\right) - 2\left(-\frac{7}{2}\right) =$

    a. -9

    b. -4

    c. 3

    d. 4

23. A game is played with an eight-component spinner with labeled with the numbers 1 through 8. A player receives two marbles each time the arrow lands on a 2 or 3, four marbles each time the arrow lands on the 6, eight marbles each time the arrow lands on a 7 or 8, and no marbles when the arrow lands on any of the other options. What is the expected value for the number of marbles that a player will receive on one spin?

    a. 3

    b. 5

    c. 15

    d. 24

24. Which of the following is equivalent to $\left(\sqrt[3]{x^4}\right)^5$?

    a. $x^{\frac{12}{5}}$

    b. $x^{\frac{15}{4}}$

    c. $x^{\frac{20}{3}}$

    d. x^{60}

25. If $x > 2$, then $\left(\frac{x^2-5x+6}{x+1}\right) \times \left(\frac{x+1}{x-2}\right) =$

   a. $x + 1$
   b. $x - 3$
   c. $\frac{x^2+2x+1}{x-2}$
   d. $\frac{x^2-2x-3}{x+1}$

26. Kyle bats third in the batting order for the Badgers baseball team. The table below shows the number of hits that Kyle had in each of 7 consecutive games played during one week in July.

Day	Monday	Tuesday	Wednesday	Thursday	Friday	Saturday	Sunday
Hits	1	2	3	1	1	4	2

What is the mean of the numbers in the distribution shown in the table?

   a. 1
   b. 2
   c. 3
   d. 4

27. $|x| > x$ for what values of x?

   a. $x < 0$
   b. $x > 0$
   c. $|x| > x$ for all real values of x.
   d. There is no real number x such that $|x| > x$.

28. Consider the following graphic showing demographics of a high school with 1219 total students:

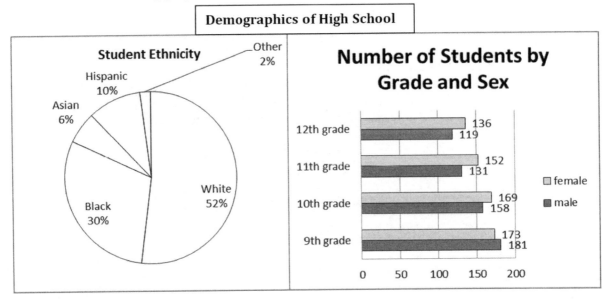

Which of these is the least quantity?

   a. The average number of Black students in the 9th and 10th grades
   b. The number of Asian female students at the school
   c. The difference in the number of male and female students at the school
   d. The difference in the number of 10th and 12th grade students at the school

- 18 -

29. $\left(\sqrt{2} + \sqrt{3}\right) \times \left(2 + \sqrt{6}\right) = ?$

    a. $2\sqrt{6} + 4$
    b. $3\sqrt{2} + 2\sqrt{3}$
    c. $5\sqrt{2} + 4\sqrt{3}$
    d. $2\sqrt{5} + \sqrt{30}$

30. A random sample of 90 students at an elementary school were asked these three questions:

    Do you like carrots?
    Do you like broccoli?
    Do you like cauliflower?

The results of the survey are shown below. If these data are representative of the population of students at the school, which of these is most probable?

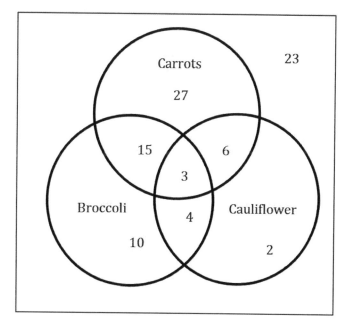

    a. A student chosen at random likes broccoli.
    b. If a student chosen at random likes carrots, he also likes at least one other vegetable.
    c. If a student chosen at random likes cauliflower and broccoli, he also likes carrots.
    d. A student chosen at random does not like carrots, broccoli, or cauliflower.

31. The formula for the volume of a pyramid is $\frac{1}{3}Bh$, where B is the area of the base and h is the height. The Pyramid of Khafre in Giza has a square base about 700 feet on a side and is about 450 feet high. Which of the following is closest to its volume?

    a. 18 million cubic feet
    b. 55 million cubic feet
    c. 75 million cubic feet
    d. 220 million cubic feet

32. In an election in Kimball County, Candidate A obtained 36,800 votes. His opponent, Candidate B, obtained 32,100 votes. 2,100 votes went to write-in candidates. What percentage of the vote went to Candidate A?

    a. 51.8%
    b. 53.4%
    c. 52.6%
    d. 46.8%

33. What is $\frac{x^3+2x}{x+3}$ when $= -1$?

    a. $-\frac{3}{2}$
    b. $-\frac{2}{3}$
    c. $\frac{1}{2}$
    d. $\frac{3}{4}$

34. A reporter for a school newspaper surveys the students at the school to ask if they prefer chocolate, vanilla, or strawberry ice cream. Of the students who answer her question, 35% prefer vanilla, and 40% prefer chocolate. What percent of the students she surveyed prefer strawberry?

    a. 15%
    b. 25%
    c. 45%
    d. There is not enough information to say.

35. A certain exam has 30 questions. A student gets 1 point for each question he gets right and loses half a point for a question he answers incorrectly; he neither gains nor loses any points for a question left blank. If C is the number of questions a student gets right and B is the number of questions he leaves blank, which of the following represents his score on the exam?

    a. $C - \frac{1}{2}B$
    b. $C - \frac{1}{2}(30 - B)$
    c. $C - \frac{1}{2}(30 - B - C)$
    d. $(30 - C) - \frac{1}{2}(30 - B)$

36. Freshmen and sophomore students at a high school were asked which caffeinated beverage they prefer. Given the two-way frequency table shown below with a summary of their responses, what is the probability that a student is a sophomore OR prefers lattes?

	Cappuccino	Latte	Frappuccino	Total
Freshman	20	29	22	71
Sophomore	19	26	22	67
Total	39	55	44	138

    a. $\frac{48}{59}$
    b. $\frac{37}{51}$
    c. $\frac{48}{69}$
    d. $\frac{39}{50}$

37. $\frac{|2|+|-2|}{|3|-|-1|} =$

    a. 0

    b. 1

    c. 2

    d. 4

38. $\frac{x^2}{y^2} + \frac{x}{y^3} =$

    a. $\frac{x^3+x}{y^3}$

    b. $\frac{x^2+xy}{y^3}$

    c. $\frac{x^2y+xy}{y^3}$

    d. $\frac{x^2y+x}{y^3}$

39. The numbers of volunteers in different states (Texas and New Mexico) for 15 different events are shown in the table below. If the following data are representative of the volunteering patterns of both states, which of the following statistics would be least helpful in determining the number of lunches that might be needed to feed the volunteers at the next event?

TX	8	17	18	19	20	21	21	21	22	28	29	31	41	45	52
NM	7	11	15	28	29	30	31	33	34	36	37	42	44	44	45

    a. Mode

    b. Mean

    c. Median

    d. Standard Deviation

40. Every person attending a certain meeting hands out a business card to every other person at the meeting. If there are a total of 30 cards handed out, how many people are at the meeting?

    a. 5

    b. 6

    c. 10

    d. 15

Advanced Algebra and Functions

Solve the following problems and select your answer from the choices given. You may use the paper you have been given for scratch paper.

41. What is the area of a parallelogram with vertices (0,0), (4,5), (10,7), and (6,2)?

    a. 20

    b. 22

    c. 24

    d. 26

    e. 28

42. If $3^x = 2$, then $x =$

    a. 9

    b. $\sqrt{3}$

    c. $\sqrt[3]{2}$

    d. $\log_3 2$

    e. $\log_2 3$

43. Which of these is described by the equation $9x^2 + 6xy + y^2 - 5x + y = 13$?

    a. An ellipse

    b. A parabola

    c. A hyperbola

    d. A spiral

    e. Two parallel lines

44. If $f(x) = \tan(2x + 4)$, then $f^{-1}(x) =$

    a. $\tan^{-1}(2x + 4)$

    b. $\sec(2x + 4)$

    c. $\tan^{-1}\left(\frac{1}{2}x - 2\right)$

    d. $2\tan^{-1}(x) - 4$

    e. $\frac{1}{2}\tan^{-1}(x) - 2$

45. $\sqrt[5]{\left(\sqrt[8]{9^{10}}\right)^6} =$

    a. 1

    b. 3

    c. $3\sqrt{3}$

    d. 27

    e. 81

46. $|6 + 2i| =$

    a. $2\sqrt{3}$

    b. $2\sqrt{10}$

    c. 6

    d. 8

    e. 12

47. A certain rectangular room is twice as wide as it is tall, and three times as long as it is wide. If the room has a volume of 12,000 ft³, what is its width?

    a. 10 ft.

    b. 12 ft.

    c. 20 ft.

    d. 30 ft.

    e. $10\sqrt[3]{12}$ ft.

48. When $(a + 2b)^5$ is expanded into a polynomial, which of the following terms does *not* appear?

    a. a^5
    b. $10a^4b$
    c. $32b^5$
    d. $40ab^4$
    e. $80a^2b^3$

49. Which of the following is equivalent to $\ln 7 + \ln 5 - \ln 3$?

    a. $\ln 4$
    b. $\ln 9$
    c. $\ln \frac{35}{3}$
    d. $\log_3 12$
    e. $\log_7 2$

50. If $\sec \theta = 2$, then which of the following is a possible value for $\sin \theta$?

    a. $-\frac{\sqrt{3}}{2}$
    b. $-\frac{1}{2}$
    c. 0
    d. 1
    e. $\frac{\sqrt{2}}{2}$

51. Which of the following is the correct graph of the system of inequalities below?

$$x - y > 1$$

$$2x + y > 2$$

a. 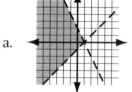   b.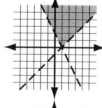

c. 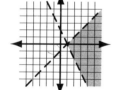   d.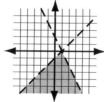

e.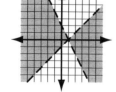

52. If $f(x) = 2x - 3$, $g(x) = x + \frac{3}{2}$, and $f(g(z)) = 6$, then $z =$

   a. -3
   b. -1
   c. 0
   d. 1
   e. 3

53. $1 + \frac{2}{3} + \frac{4}{9} + \frac{8}{27} + \cdots =$

   a. 3
   b. π
   c. 3π
   d. 9
   e. ∞

54. Which of the following matrices is *not* invertible?

   a. $\begin{bmatrix} 1 & 2 \\ 3 & 6 \end{bmatrix}$
   b. $\begin{bmatrix} 1 & 2 \\ 3 & 0 \end{bmatrix}$
   c. $\begin{bmatrix} 1 & 3 \\ 6 & 2 \end{bmatrix}$
   d. $\begin{bmatrix} 1 & 2 \\ 6 & 3 \end{bmatrix}$
   e. $\begin{bmatrix} 2 & 3 \\ 1 & 6 \end{bmatrix}$

55. A drawer contains eight pairs of socks. If Susan chooses four socks at random from the drawer, what are the chances that she will get two left socks and two right socks?

   a. 1/2
   b. 2/5
   c. 1/64
   d. 28/65
   e. 56/143

56. $\left(2 + \sqrt{3}\right) \div \left(2 - \sqrt{3}\right) =$

   a. 2
   b. $\sqrt{3}$
   c. 7
   d. $1 + 4\sqrt{3}$
   e. $7 + 4\sqrt{3}$

57. The half-life of the isotope ^{226}Ra is about 1,600 years. A certain sample of rock contains two grams of radioactive ^{226}Ra. How much did it contain 8,000 years ago?

   a. 0.4 g
   b. 5 g
   c. 10 g
   d. 20 g
   e. 64 g

58. Which of the following lines includes a diameter of the circle $(x - 1)^2 + (y - 2)^2 = 4$?

a. $y = x - \frac{1}{2}$

b. $y = 2x + 2$

c. $y = 2x + 4$

d. $y = 3x - 1$

e. $y = 4x + 2$

59. Sylvia, who is just over five feet tall, stands 195 feet away from the base of a tower and looks toward the top of the tower with a 45° angle of inclination. Approximately how tall is the tower?

a. 100 ft.

b. 200 ft.

c. 400 ft.

d. $200\sqrt{3}$ ft.

e. $400\sqrt{3}$ ft.

60. If $p^q = r$, then which of the following is equivalent to q?

a. $p \ln r$

b. $r \ln p$

c. $\dfrac{\ln r}{\ln p}$

d. $\dfrac{\ln p}{\ln r}$

e. $\log_r p$

- 25 -

Answer Explanations #1

Reading

1. B: There is no indication in the passage that the Bennets are interested in becoming friends with Mr. Bingley (choice A), that Mr. Bingley would be a valuable business connection (choice C), or that Mr. Bingley has any prior knowledge of the Bennet daughters (choice D). Mrs. Bennet tells her husband that a new neighbor is moving in: "Mrs. Long says that Netherfield is taken by a young man of large fortune." Mrs. Bennet is sure he will make an excellent husband for one of her daughters: "You must know that I am thinking of his marrying one of them."

2. B: Mrs. Bennet is annoyed and fed up with her husband's seeming indifference to Mr. Bingley: "'My dear Mr. Bennet,' replied his wife, 'how can you be so tiresome!'"

3. B: The evidence in this selection indicates that marrying a man with money was a primary goal for young women. Mrs. Bennet tells Mr. Bennet that Mr. Bingley is "A single man of large fortune; four or five thousand a year." Mrs. Bennet further indicates that she is thrilled with the news because of Mr. Bingley's potential as a husband for one of her daughters: "What a fine thing for our girls... You must know that I am thinking of his marrying one of them."

4. A: Mr. Bennet is facetiously asking if the idea of marriage (particularly to one of his own daughters) was Mr. Bingley's intention when he agreed to rent Netherfield Park.

5. B: The entire passage makes the argument that Black History Month should be abolished, offering various reasons why this is the best course of action.

6. D: The context of the sentence suggests that post-racial refers to an approach in which race is not a useful or positive organizing principle.

7. D: Clearly both authors think it is important for students to learn about the achievements and experience of African Americans; their debate is whether observing Black History Month is the best way to achieve this goal.

8. C: The author of Passage 2 points out that just because there is a month focused on African American history, this doesn't mean that African American history must be ignored for the rest of the year.

9. B: Answer choice (B) accurately provides an inference that has clear antecedent in the passage. The author of the passage claims, "By the Middle Ages, this came to be recognized as the diamond. Over time, the legendary adamant came to take on a mystical quality that passed into certain forms of medieval literature and, even today, has an allegorical place in some genres." This means that the inference and claim made in answer choice (B) are correct: the adamant *was* originally associated with mythical qualities, and as a result writers still utilize it in literature for its figurative (or allegorical) attributes. Answer choice (B) is correct.

10. D: At the end of the passage, the author notes, "Men carry a single X chromosome, possessing an XY-chromosome makeup, while women carry two X chromosomes, thus having the potential to combat colorblindness with an extra X chromosome." This suggests that men are more likely to be colorblind than women because men have only a single X chromosome. Of all the answer choices, answer choice (D) can best be inferred from the passage, so it is correct.

11. C: is the correct answer because paragraph 7 mostly gives specific details showing how far away Alaska is from the mainland (such as in the phrase that says *they were yet less than half way*). Choice A is incorrect because the group is not yet in Alaska. Instead, they are journeying towards the territory and learning how big it is. Although the paragraph does give some details about people in the group, such as the hometown of some of the travelers, the majority of the paragraph focuses on the location and size of Alaska. Choice D is incorrect because this just a detail listed at the end of the paragraph. The main part of the paragraph talks about the size and distance of the territory.

12. C: The author states early in the passage, "the piano is an instrument that knows no one age for learning and presents multiple opportunities for the successful attainment of musical skills." This suggests that the piano is *one* instrument that both adults and children can learn to play. This does not imply, however, that the piano is the *only* instrument that adults and children can learn to play. Answer choice (C) cannot be concluded from the passage, so it is the correct answer.

13. D: Of all the answer choices, answer choice (D) is the only one that can correctly be inferred from the information in the passage. The author states that "little plant growth will be able to survive" in Iceland, that "plants require a long period of time to grow in Iceland," and that "the plant life in Iceland is also notoriously delicate." This suggests that off-road vehicles have the potential to destroy plant life, leaving plants unable to grow back for long periods of time or, in some cases, unable to grow back at all. Therefore, answer choice (D) is correct.

14. D: Answer choice (D) most clearly explains the reason for the farmer's concerns about cost. Although the cost of supplies and maintenance might be lower than that of a non-organic farm, the cost of the certification itself is very high, creating a financial burden for the farmer as he tries to establish the certified organic farm. Answer choice (D) is correct.

15. D: is the best choice because it best summarizes the thoughts in paragraph 7. A, B, and C are not the best choices because they do not accurately and completely summarize the thoughts expressed in paragraph 7.

16. B: The author describes the history of the islands and gives informative details about the islands and the people who lived there in the past. Choice A is incorrect because the author does not make jokes during the article; instead, he simply describes facts. Choice C is incorrect because the author does not display anger or any other emotions; he simply describes facts. Choice D is incorrect because the author proves that he's very interested in the topic by giving many descriptive details. Therefore, he is the opposite of bored.

17. A: The passage is a broad overview of single-pilot resource management (SRM).

18. D: "Short on money" is a clue that Glenda could not afford new appliances. Sufficient means adequate or tolerable. If Glenda is not able to buy new appliances, then her current appliances will have to be satisfactory until she can afford new appliances.

19. B: *Culminate* means to come to completion. The words "perfect season" and "championship win" allude to the happy ending of the basketball season. *Culminate* is the only choice that fits.

20. D: The only two word choices which make any sense at all are subside and intensify. The next day's light breezes indicate that the winds would decrease, or subside, making subside the best choice. While it is possible that the already high winds could intensify, it is far more likely that the "light breezes" indicate that they did the opposite.

Writing

1. A: The sentence as written is a fact that is not essential to this passage. To maintain the focus of the passage, the author should note a reason for including this information. Choice A is the best option because the fact remains and the focus can continue with explaining the reason for the importance of the lyrics. Choice B is not the best option because it is not the focus of the passage on whether the song is popular. Instead, the focus is on how the song is impactful to an individual. Choice C is not the option because it does not correct the shift in focus. Choice D is not correct because the sentence should be revised.

2. C: because the missing verb in this sentence must have something to do with possession, since it discusses the band's success. *Had* indicates possession. A, B, and D are incorrect, because these verbs do not fit within the sentence.

3. A: because the sentence is missing the article *as*. This is the simplest way to express the idea of the sentence. B is incorrect because this sentence is not grammatically correct. C is incorrect because the first sentence is grammatically incorrect.

4. B: because this is the simplest way to express the idea in a grammatically correct sentence. A is incorrect because a comma is missing after *song* and after *people*. C is incorrect because a comma is missing after *song*, and quotation marks are missing around the quotation, *"Imagine all the people."* D is not correct. A comma is missing after *song* and after *people*, and quotation marks are missing around the quotation, *"Imagine all the people."*

5. C: because in this sentence *nice* is an adjective rather than an adverb. It describes the noun, *sounds*, not the verb. A is not correct. *When I really listen to the words of this song* is an introductory clause, and a comma is needed after the clause. B is not correct. *Something* is one word when used as a noun. D is not correct. Although most of the essay is in the past tense, the final paragraph is in the present tense. *Realized* is in the past tense.

6. B: It is correct because a comma is needed to separate the interjection of the book title. A is not correct. Ship in the sentence is possessive and requires the apostrophe. C is not correct. Are is the plural of is. The subject, events, is plural and therefore the verb needs to be plural in subject-verb agreement. D is not correct. Are brought is in the past participle, and bring is in the present tense.

7. D: It is correct because were is the plural past tense of is. The subject of the sentence, lifeboats, is plural, and the verb also must be plural in subject-verb agreement. A is not correct. There is used correctly. They're is a contraction of they are. B is not correct. A comma is needed to separate the interjection, and as a result. C is not correct. Lifeboats is not possessive and does not require the apostrophe.

8. B: It is correct because there is no need for a comma. As it stands, the comma disrupts the normal flow of thought in the sentence. A is not correct. The subject, ship, is singular, and the verb also must be singular in subject-verb agreement. C is not correct. Was divided is in the past participle. Divide is in the present tense, and the rest of the essay is in the past.

9. B: It is correct because it is the simplest way to express the idea in a grammatically correct sentence. Because of this refers to the content of the previous sentence. A is not correct. This sentence is not grammatically correct. C is not correct. This sentence is not grammatically correct. D is not correct. This sentence is not grammatically correct and needs a comma after class.

10. C: It is correct because it connects the ideas from the previous sentence with the current sentence. The previous sentences explained the relationship between the locations of rooms to the deck with the survival rate of passengers. Sentence 13 provides additional information on this subject. A is not correct. Lastly is not an appropriate transition word as there was not a series of listed facts. B is not correct. However is not an appropriate transition word because sentence 13 is not contradicting anything from the previous sentence. D is not correct. Therefore is not an appropriate transition word because the new information does not involve cause and effect with the previous sentences.

11. D: This is the best combination of all the information provided by the author and maintains the author's original meaning. The other choices delete information that was provided by the author and change the author's original meaning.

12. D: The word "it's" in this sentence is used incorrectly, because it is a contraction of "it is", which makes no sense. The word should be "its", which is a possessive pronoun.

13. B: In the first clause of sentence 8, "teams" is plural, so it must have a plural verb to go with it. So "was" needs to be changed to "were."

14. C: Switching sentences 11 and 12 improves the organization and clarity of paragraph 3.

15. B: The word "its" in this sentence is used incorrectly, because it is actually a possessive pronoun. The word needed is "it's", which is a contraction of "it is."

16. D: Sentence 4 is already in its best place for this passage. Following sentence 3, the fourth sentence provides a needed example. So, it is best served in its current place.

17. B: This is the best choice because it transitions correctly from sentence 7 to sentence 8 and maintains the author's original meaning.

18. C: In terms of determining their validity, hypotheses are confirmed or disconfirmed. None of the other options are meaningful.

19. D: Since the sentence begins in the present tense, it should continue in the present tense as well. The proper verb to be used in this clause is *affect*, meaning to have an impact, not *effect*, meaning to bring about.

20. B: The second sentence of the same last passage paragraph states, "In the monkey example, every single monkey in the history of monkeys would need to be examined before the hypothesis could be proven or disproven." In the last passage sentence, "...infinite sample sets for confirmation or disconfirmation" refers directly to that second sentence (quoted above here). The initial sentence of this paragraph (a) states that evidence-based hypotheses must use probability because sample sets are too large, which agrees with the sentence following it, but does not specifically identify infinite sample sets as that second sentence following it does. The fourth sentence of the previous paragraph (c) shows how even one piece of evidence out of a very large—but NOT infinite—sample size of one billion can disprove a hypothesis rather than showing how infinite sample sizes are required. Since (b) is correct, (d) is incorrect.

21. B: Although it is a simple combination, this connection of sentence 2 and sentence 3 is the one that remains grammatically correct, maintains the author's original intent, and is logical.

22. D: A past tense verb is needed for this sentence.

23. C: The passage speaks of New Zealand being colonized, where previously it was not occupied, so incursion is not an accurate word to describe the coming of the settlers. Influx is a more appropriate description.

24. D: This is the best choice because it transitions correctly from sentence 9 to sentence 10 and maintains the author's original meaning.

25. D: Sentence 18 functions best in its current place as sentence 16 functions as a topic sentence on the sweet potato, and sentence 18 logically comes after sentence 17 stating how the sweet potato could grow in many areas and survive the winter months as well.

Mathematics

Arithmetic

1. B: To convert an improper fraction to a mixed number, divide the numerator by the denominator: the quotient is the integer part of the mixed number, and the remainder is the numerator. $27 \div 8 = 3$ with a remainder of 3, so $\frac{27}{8} = 3\frac{3}{8}$.

2. A: In order to subtract decimal numbers, write them one above the other with the decimal points aligned, filling in zeroes as necessary, and then carry out the subtraction normally, placing the decimal point in the same position in the result:

$$6.32$$

$$-\underline{3.50}$$

$$2.82$$

3. D: The volume of a right rectangular prism—that is, a box shape—is equal to the product of its length, width, and height. So the volume of the given box is equal to $(20 \text{ cm})(30 \text{ cm})(15 \text{ cm}) = 9,000 \text{ cm}^3$.

4. B: Recalling that percent just means "divided by 100," each of the given numbers can be represented as fractions:

I. $0.071\% = \frac{0.071}{100} = \frac{71}{100,000}$, II. $0.71 = \frac{71}{100}$, III. $7.1\% = \frac{7.1}{100} = \frac{71}{1,000}$, IV. $\frac{71}{101}$

All of the fractions share the same numerator. Among fractions with the same numerator, the largest fraction has the smallest denominator. We can order these fractions from greatest to least by ordering the denominators from least to greatest. The correct order is $\frac{71}{100} > \frac{71}{101} > \frac{71}{1,000} > \frac{71}{100,000}$ which corresponds to choice B.

5. B: The number of people who voted for the proposition is 9.5% of 51,623. If we only require an approximation, we can round 9.5% to 10%, and 51,623 to 50,000. Then 9.5% of 51,623 is about 10% of 50,000, or $(0.1)(50,000) = 5,000$.

6. D: In mathematics, the word "of" indicates multiplication. So $\frac{5}{6}$ of $\frac{3}{4}$ is just $\frac{5}{6} \times \frac{3}{4} = \frac{5 \times 3}{6 \times 4} = \frac{15}{24}$, which reduces to $\frac{15 \div 3}{24 \div 3} = \frac{5}{8}$.

7. D: If there are three feet in a yard, then to convert yards to feet we just multiply by 3. So five yards is equal to $5 \times 3 = 15$ feet. Likewise, since there are twelve inches in a foot, to convert feet to inches, we just multiply by 12. So 15 feet is equal to $15 \times 12 = 180$ inches.

8. B: To multiply decimals, first multiply the numbers normally ignoring the decimal point; then, position the decimal point in the answer so that the number of digits after the decimal point in the product is equal to the *sum* of the number of digits after the decimal point in both factors. Performing the multiplication without regard to the decimal point first, we get $22 \times 313 = 6886$. Since there is one digit after the decimal point in 2.2 and one digit after the decimal point in 31.3, there should be two digits after the decimal point in the product, which is therefore 68.86.

9. D: To find the average of a set of numbers, add the numbers together and divide by how many there are (in this case, three). So, to find the average of $\frac{1}{3}, \frac{2}{3}$, and $\frac{1}{4}$, we first add them together. To add fractions, we can convert them all to fractions which have the least common denominator, which is in this case 12: $\frac{1}{3} + \frac{2}{3} + \frac{1}{4} = \frac{1 \times 4}{3 \times 4} + \frac{2 \times 4}{3 \times 4} + \frac{1 \times 3}{4 \times 3} = \frac{4}{12} + \frac{8}{12} + \frac{3}{12} = \frac{4+8+3}{12} = \frac{15}{12}$, which reduces to $\frac{15 \div 3}{12 \div 3} = \frac{5}{4}$. To get the average, we now divide this sum by three: $\frac{5}{4} \div 3 = \frac{5}{4} \times \frac{1}{3} = \frac{5 \times 1}{4 \times 3} = \frac{5}{12}$.

10. D: When comparing fractions it is necessary to find common denominators.

A. $\frac{49}{56} = \frac{7}{8} < \frac{6}{7} = \frac{48}{56}$

B. $\frac{108}{120} = \frac{9}{10} > \frac{11}{12} = \frac{110}{120}$

C. $\frac{26}{39} = \frac{2}{3} > \frac{9}{13} = \frac{27}{39}$

D. $\frac{7}{28} = \frac{1}{4} < \frac{2}{7} = \frac{8}{28}$ <Correct>

Once all of the fractions have been represented using common denominators, it is easy to determine which of each pair is greater since the greater is the one with the larger numerator. Among the four choices, the only valid inequality is choice D.

11. A: To convert a number to scientific notation, move the decimal point until there is just one digit before it (not counting leading zeroes), and rewrite the number as the result times a power of ten. The exponent of the power of ten is equal to the number of places the decimal point was moved—positive if the decimal was moved left, and negative if the decimal was moved right. Starting with 0.0023, to put only one digit before the decimal point, we have to move the decimal point three places to the right. Therefore, $0.0023 = 2.3 \times 10^{-3}$.

12. B: Since all students who answered her survey said they prefer one of the three flavors, the percentages must add up to 100%. Therefore the percentage of students who prefer strawberry must be $100\% - (35\% + 40\%) = 100\% - 75\% = 25\%$.

13. C: To find out how much more milk he needs, subtract the amount he has from the amount he needs: $2\frac{1}{4} - 1\frac{1}{2}$. To add or subtract mixed numbers, first convert them to improper fractions. We can do this by multiplying the integer part by the denominator and adding that to the numerator. So, $2\frac{1}{4} = \frac{2 \times 4 + 1}{4} = \frac{9}{4}$, and $1\frac{1}{2} = \frac{1 \times 2 + 1}{2} = \frac{3}{2}$. Now convert both fractions so that they share the lowest common denominator, which in this case is 4. $\frac{9}{4}$ already has a denominator of 4, so we need to convert $\frac{3}{2}$: $\frac{3}{2} = \frac{3 \times 2}{2 \times 2} = \frac{6}{4}$. We can now subtract: $\frac{9}{4} - \frac{6}{4} = \frac{3}{4}$.

14. B: 15,012 is close to 15,000, and 19,938 is close to 20,000. We would therefore expect $\frac{15,012}{19,938}$ to be close to $\frac{15,000}{20,000} = \frac{15}{20} = \frac{15 \div 5}{20 \div 5} = \frac{3}{4}$.

15. A: To multiply a fraction by a decimal, it is helpful to either convert both numbers to decimals or both to fractions. If we convert $\frac{2}{5}$ to a fraction, we divide 2 by 5, putting a decimal point after the 2 and keeping track of where the digits of the quotient are relative to the decimal point:

$$
\begin{array}{r}
.4 \\
5\overline{)2.0} \\
2\,0 \\
\hline
0
\end{array}
$$

So $\frac{2}{5} = 0.4$, and $\frac{2}{5} \times 2.5 = 0.4 \times 2.5$. $4 \times 25 = 100$, and since 0.4 and 2.5 each have one digit after the decimal point, the product should have two digits after the decimal point, so the answer is 1.00, or simply 1.

Alternately, if we convert 2.5 to a fraction, we can write $2.5 = 2 + 0.5 = 2 + \frac{5}{10} = 2 + \frac{1}{2} = \frac{5}{2}$. Then, $\frac{2}{5} \times \frac{5}{2} = \frac{2 \times 5}{5 \times 2} = \frac{10}{10} = 1$.

16. A: It is helpful to put the expressions in similar terms. In this case, all of the options can be expressed in terms of 3.

A. $\left(\frac{1}{3}\right)^{-4} = 3^4$

B. $9^{\frac{3}{2}} = 3^3$

C. $27^{\frac{2}{3}} = (3^3)^{\frac{2}{3}} = 3^2$

D. $3^{-\frac{25}{3}} = \left(\frac{1}{3}\right)^{\frac{25}{3}} < 1$

The first three options are powers of 3 of which choice A is the highest (positive) power and hence represents the largest number. Choice C is a negative power that indicates the positive power is associated with the reciprocal of the base value. In this case, 3 to a negative power is equivalent to 1/3 to the corresponding positive power. Any number less than one to a positive power greater than 1 is a number less than 1.

17. A: To find Sam's average speed, we have to divide the total distance he travelled by the total travel time. Note that fifteen minutes is a quarter hour, and forty-five minutes is $\frac{3}{4}$ hours. During the first fifteen minutes, therefore, the distance Sam runs is 8 mph $\times \frac{1}{4}$ hour = 2 miles. During the next forty-five minutes, he jogs 4 mph $\times \frac{3}{4}$ hours = 3 miles. So, the total distance he runs is $2 + 3 = 5$ miles. The time he runs is $\frac{1}{4}$ hour $+ \frac{3}{4}$ hours = 1 hour, so his average speed is 5 miles / 1 hour = 5 miles per hour.

18. D: Since the five angles together go all the way around the central point, they must add up to a complete rotation of 360°. Therefore, if the angles are all equal, each angle must have a measure of $\frac{360°}{5} = 72°$.

19. B: Translate "What percent of 800 is 40?" into the mathematical equation $x\% \cdot 800 = 40$. To solve, divide 40 by 800 and convert the answer to a percent. To divide a smaller number by a larger, add a decimal point after the smaller number and add zeroes as necessary, putting the decimal point in the same position in the quotient as it appears in the dividend:

$$
\begin{array}{r}
.05 \\
800\overline{)40.00} \\
\underline{40\ 00} \\
0
\end{array}
$$

So $40 \div 800 = 0.05$. To express this as a percent, just multiply by 100, which moves the decimal point two places to the left: $0.05 = 5\%$.

20. C: To convert a fraction into a decimal, divide the numerator by the denominator. To divide a smaller number by a larger, add a decimal point after the smaller number and add zeroes as necessary, putting the decimal point in the same position in the quotient as it appears in the dividend:

$$
\begin{array}{r}
0.1875 \\
16\overline{)3.0000} \\
\underline{1\ 6} \\
1\ 40 \\
\underline{1\ 28} \\
120 \\
\underline{112} \\
80 \\
\underline{80} \\
0
\end{array}
$$

Quantitative Reasoning, Algebra, and Statistics

21. D: To simplify the inequality $3 - 2x < 5$, we can first subtract 3 from both sides: $3 - 2x - 3 < 5 - 3 \Rightarrow -2x < 2$. Now, we can divide both sides of the inequality by -2. When an inequality is multiplied or divided by a negative number, its direction changes ($<$ becomes $>$, $\leq$ becomes $\geq$, and vice versa). So $-2x < 2$ becomes $\frac{-2x}{-2} > \frac{2}{-2}$, or $x > -1$.

22. C: $6\left(-\frac{2}{3}\right) - 2\left(-\frac{7}{2}\right) = \left(\frac{6}{1}\right)\left(-\frac{2}{3}\right) - \left(\frac{2}{1}\right)\left(-\frac{7}{2}\right) = -\left(\frac{6}{1}\right)\left(\frac{2}{3}\right) - \left(-\left(\frac{2}{1}\right)\left(\frac{7}{2}\right)\right) = -\frac{6\times 2}{1\times 3} + \frac{2\times 7}{1\times 2} = -\frac{12}{3} + \frac{14}{2} = -4 + 7 = 3$.

23. A: The expected value is equal to the sum of the products of the probability and marbles won for each value of the spinner.

$$E(X) = \left(2 \cdot \frac{1}{8}\right) + \left(2 \cdot \frac{1}{8}\right) + \left(4 \cdot \frac{1}{8}\right) + \left(8 \cdot \frac{1}{8}\right) + \left(8 \cdot \frac{1}{8}\right) + \left(0 \cdot \frac{1}{8}\right) + \left(0 \cdot \frac{1}{8}\right) + \left(0 \cdot \frac{1}{8}\right)$$

$$= \frac{2}{8} + \frac{2}{8} + \frac{4}{8} + \frac{8}{8} + \frac{8}{8} + 0 + 0 + 0 = \frac{24}{8} = 3$$

24. C: The nth root of x is equivalent to x to the power of $\frac{1}{n}$, i.e. $\sqrt[n]{x} = x^{\frac{1}{n}}$. This means in particular that $\sqrt[3]{x} = x^{\frac{1}{3}}$, and so $\left(\sqrt[3]{(x^4)}\right)^5 = \left((x^4)^{\frac{1}{3}}\right)^5$. Raising a power to another power is equivalent to multiplying the exponents together, so this equals $x^{4 \times \frac{1}{3} \times 5} = x^{\frac{20}{3}}$.

25. B: $\left(\frac{x^2-5x+6}{x+1}\right) \times \left(\frac{x+1}{x-2}\right) = \frac{(x^2-5x+6) \times (x+1)}{(x+1) \times (x-2)}$. Before carrying out the multiplication of the polynomials, notice that there is a factor of $x + 1$ in both the numerator and denominator, so the expression reduces to $\frac{x^2-5x+6}{x-2}$. We can simplify further by factoring the numerator. One way to factor a quadratic expression with a leading coefficient of 1 is to look for two numbers that add to the coefficient of x (in this case -5) and multiply to the constant term (in this case 6). Two such numbers are -2 and -3: $(-2) + (-3) = -5$ and $(-2) \times (-3) = 6$. So $x^2 - 5x + 6 = (x - 2)(x - 3)$. That means $\frac{x^2-5x+6}{x-2} = \frac{(x-2)(x-3)}{x-2}$. The $x - 2$ in the numerator and denominator can cancel, so we are left with just $x - 3$. (Note that if $x = -1$ or $x = 2$, the obtained simplified expression would not be true: either value of x would result in a denominator of zero in the original expression, so the whole expression would be undefined. Therefore, it is necessary to state that these values of x are excluded from the domain. For a domain of $x > 2$, both -1 and 2 are excluded as possible values of x.)

26. G: The mean, or average, is the sum of the numbers in a data set, divided by the total number of items. This data set contains seven items, one for each day of the week. The total number of hits that Kyle had during the week is the sum of the numbers in the right-hand column, or 14. This gives

$$Mean = \frac{14}{7} = 2.$$

27. A: When $x \geq 0$, $|x| = x$, so it is not true that $|x| > x$. However, when < 0, $|x| = -x$. This means x is negative and $|x|$ is positive, and since any positive number is greater than any negative number, $|x| > x$ when $x < 0$.

28. B: The difference in the number of male and female students at the school is $630 - 589 = 41$, and the difference in the number of 9th and 12th grade students at the school is 327 – 255 = 72. There are approximately 38 Asian females at the school (0.06 * 630). The average number of black students is more than 90 (30% of 300) because there are more than 90 in the 10th grade and the class is smaller than the 9th grade group.

29. C: A method commonly taught to multiply two binomials is the "FOIL" method, an acronym for First, Outer, Inner, Last: multiply the first terms of each factor, then the outer terms, and so forth. Applied to $\left(\sqrt{2} + \sqrt{3}\right) \times (2 + \sqrt{6})$, this yields $\left(\sqrt{2}\right)(2) + \left(\sqrt{2}\right)\left(\sqrt{6}\right) + \left(\sqrt{3}\right)(2) + \left(\sqrt{3}\right)\left(\sqrt{6}\right) = 2\sqrt{2} + \sqrt{12} + 2\sqrt{3} + \sqrt{18}$. Two of these terms can be simplified: $12 = 4 \times 3$, so $\sqrt{12} = \sqrt{4} \times \sqrt{3} = 2\sqrt{3}$,

and $18 = 9 \times 2$, so $\sqrt{18} = \sqrt{9} \times \sqrt{2} = 3\sqrt{2}$. Therefore, the produce can be written as $2\sqrt{2} + 2\sqrt{3} + 2\sqrt{3} + 3\sqrt{2}$, which simplifies to $5\sqrt{2} + 4\sqrt{3}$ after like terms are combined.

30. B: The results are displayed in a Venn diagram, so to get the number of students who like any particular vegetable, sum all of the numbers that appear within the circle for that vegetable. 32 of the 90 students like broccoli, so the probability of A is $\frac{32}{90} \approx 0.356$. There are 51 students who like carrots, and of those 51, 24 also like another vegetable, so the probability of B is $\frac{24}{51} \approx 0.471$. There are 7 students who like broccoli and cauliflower, and of those 7, 3 also like carrots, so the probability of C is $\frac{3}{7} \approx 0.429$. 23 of the 90 students did not like any of the vegetables, so the probability of D is $\frac{23}{90} \approx 0.256$. B has the highest probability of these choices.

31. C: The area of the square base is just the square of the side length: $(700 \text{ ft})^2 = 490,000 \text{ ft}^2$. Since we only need an approximation, we can round that to $500,000 \text{ ft}^2$, or half a million square feet. The volume is therefore $\frac{1}{3}Bh \approx \frac{1}{3}\left(\frac{1}{2}\text{ million ft}^2\right)(450 \text{ ft}) = \frac{450}{6}\text{ million ft}^3 = 75 \text{ million ft}^3$.

32. A: Candidate A's vote percentage is determined by the number of votes that he obtained, divided by the total number of votes cast, and then multiplied by 100 to convert the decimal into a percentage. Therefore,

$$\text{Candidate A's vote percentage} = \frac{36,800}{36,800+32,100+2,100} = \frac{36,800}{71,000} = 51.8\%.$$

33. A: To evaluate $\frac{x^3+2x}{x+3}$ at $= -1$, substitute in -1 for x in the expression: $\frac{(-1)^3+2(-1)}{(-1)+3} = \frac{(-1)+(-2)}{2} = \frac{-3}{2} = -\frac{3}{2}$.

34. B: Since all students who answered her survey said they prefer one of the three flavors, the percentages must add up to 100%. Therefore the percentage of students who prefer strawberry must be $100\% - (35\% + 40\%) = 100\% - 75\% = 25\%$.

35. C: If the exam has 30 questions, and the student answered C questions correctly and left B questions blank, then the number of questions the student answered incorrectly must be $30 - B - C$. He gets one point for each correct question, or $1 \times C = C$ points, and loses $\frac{1}{2}$ point for each incorrect question, or $\frac{1}{2}(30 - B - C)$ points. Therefore, one way to express his total score is $C - \frac{1}{2}(30 - B - C)$

36. C: We can find the probability by adding the distinct probabilities that a given student is a sophomore and that a given student prefers lattes. However, we must also remember to subtract off the probabilities that a student is a Sophomore AND prefers lattes. Our previous calculation double counted these students. The probability may be written as: $P(S \text{ or } L) = \frac{67}{138} + \frac{55}{138} - \frac{26}{138}$. Thus, the probability a student is a Sophomore or prefers Lattes is $\frac{48}{69}$.

37. C: $|-2| = |2| = 2$, $|3| = 3$, and $|-1| = 1$. So $\frac{|2|+|-2|}{|3|-|-1|} = \frac{2+2}{3-1} = \frac{4}{2} = 2$.

38. D: To add the two fractions, first rewrite them with the least common denominator, which is in this case y^3. $\frac{x}{y^3}$ already has this denominator, and we can rewrite $\frac{x^2}{y^2}$ as $\frac{x^2 \times y}{y^2 \times y} = \frac{x^2 y}{y^3}$. Thus, $\frac{x^2}{y^2} + \frac{x}{y^3} = \frac{x^2 y}{y^3} + \frac{x}{y^3} = \frac{x^2 y + x}{y^3}$.

39. A: The Mean and Median both offer insight into how many volunteers to expect. The standard deviation would give an idea as to how much that number may vary. The mode is the least helpful. For example in this case, although the Texas mode (21) reasonably represents its data, the New Mexico mode (44) is not a good representation of the data set.

40. B: Call the number of people present at the meeting x. If each person hands out a card to every *other* person (that is, every person besides himself), then each person hands out $x - 1$ cards. The total number of cards handed out is therefore $(x - 1)$. Since we are told there are a total of 30 cards handed out, we have the equation $(x - 1) = 30$, which we can rewrite as the quadratic equation $x^2 - x - 30 = 0$. We can solve this equation by factoring the quadratic expression. One way to do this is to find two numbers that add to the coefficient of x (in this case -1) and that multiply to the constant term (in this case -30). Those two numbers are 5 and -6. Our factored equation is therefore $(x + 5)(x - 6) = 0$. To make the equation true, one or both of the factors must be zero: either $+5 = 0$, in which case $x = -5$, or $x - 6 = 0$, in which case $x = 6$. Obviously the number of people at the meeting cannot be negative, so the second solution, $x = 6$, must be correct.

Advanced Algebra and Functions

41. B: The area of the parallelogram can be determined in several ways. Recall that the area of a parallelogram is equal to the magnitude of the cross product of the vectors representing two adjacent sides. We can express the side connecting the points $(0, 0)$ and $(4, 5)$ as the vector $(4 - 0, 5 - 0) = (4, 5)$ and the side connecting the points $(0, 0)$ and $(6, 2)$ as the vector $(6 - 0, 2 - 0) = (6, 2)$. For two vectors in the xy plane (u_1, v_1) and (u_2, v_2), the magnitude of the cross product is $|u_1 v_2 - u_2 v_1|$, which in this case would be $|4 \times 2 - 6 \times 5| = |-22| = 22$.

42. D: To solve the equation $3^x = 2$, we need to take the logarithm base three of both sides of the equation. (b^x and $\log_b x$ are inverse functions and cancel each other out for any positive base b.) Then we have $\log_3(3^x) = \log_3 2$, or simply $x = \log_3 2$. Alternatively, just keep in mind that $a^b = c$ is equivalent to $\log_a c = b$ for any positive a and c, so $3^x = 2$ is equivalent to $\log_3 2 = x$.

43. B: In general, any equation of the form $Ax^2 + Bxy + Cy^2 + Dx + Ey + F = 0$ describes a (possibly degenerate) conic section. (In the given equation, the constant term is on the right-hand side of the equation, but that's unimportant; we can easily convert it to the above form by simply subtracting 13 from both sides.) To determine which kind of conic section the equation corresponds to, we can look at the discriminant, $B^2 - 4AC$. If the discriminant is positive, the equation represents a hyperbola, if the discriminant is negative, the equation represents an ellipse or circle; and if the discriminant is zero, the equation represents a parabola. Here the discriminant is $6^2 - 4(9)(1) = 36 - 36 = 0$, so the equation represents a parabola.

44. E: One way to find an inverse function is to take the original equation describing the function, replace $f(x)$ with x and x with $f^{-1}(x)$, and then solve for $f^{-1}(x)$. In this case, $f(x) = \tan(2x + 4)$ becomes $x = \tan(2f^{-1}(x) + 4)$. To solve for $f^{-1}(x)$, first take the inverse tangent of both sides: $\tan^{-1} x = \tan^{-1}(\tan(2f^{-1}(x) + 4)) = 2f^{-1}(x) + 4$. Now subtract four from both sides: $\tan^{-1} x - 4 = 2f^{-1}(x)$. Finally, divide both sides by 2: $\frac{1}{2}(\tan^{-1} x - 4) = f^{-1}(x)$, or $f^{-1}(x) = \frac{1}{2}\tan^{-1} x - 2$.

45. D: $\sqrt[n]{x}$ is equivalent to $x^{\frac{1}{n}}$, so $\sqrt[5]{\left(\sqrt[8]{9^{10}}\right)^6}$ can be rewritten as $\left(\left((9^{10})^{\frac{1}{8}}\right)^6\right)^{\frac{1}{5}}$. When raising a power to another power, the exponents multiply, so this is equivalent to $9^{10\times\frac{1}{8}\times6\times\frac{1}{5}}$. $10 \times \frac{1}{8} \times 6 \times \frac{1}{5} = \frac{10}{1} \times \frac{1}{8} \times \frac{6}{1} \times \frac{1}{5} = \frac{10\times1\times6\times1}{5\times1\times8\times1} = \frac{60}{40}$, which reduces to $\frac{3}{2}$. The original expression therefore reduces to $9^{\frac{3}{2}}$, which is equal to $\left(\sqrt{9}\right)^3 = 3^3 = 27$.

46. B: The absolute value of a complex number $a + bi$ is equal to $\sqrt{a^2 + b^2}$. $|6 + 2i|$ is therefore $\sqrt{6^2 + 2^2} = \sqrt{36 + 4} = \sqrt{40} = \sqrt{4} \times \sqrt{10} = 2\sqrt{10}$.

47. C: The volume of a rectangular solid is the product of its length, width, and height, $= l \times w \times h$. In this case, we're told the room is twice as wide as it is tall, and three times as long as it is wide, so we can write $w = 2h$ — or, equivalently, $h = \frac{w}{2}$ —and $l = 3w$. Our volume equation then becomes $V = 3w \times w \times \frac{w}{2} = \frac{3}{2}w^3$. Setting that equal to the given volume of 12,000 ft³, we have $\frac{3}{2}w^3 = 12,000$, so $w^3 = \frac{2}{3} \times 12,000 = 8,000$, and $w = \sqrt[3]{8,000} = 20$ ft.

48. D: A power of a binomial can be expanded by the binomial theorem, $(x + y)^n = \sum_{i=0}^{n} \binom{n}{i} x^{n-i}y^i$, where $\binom{n}{i}$ is the binomial coefficient, which can be derived either from Pascal's triangle or from the equation $\binom{n}{i} = \frac{n!}{i!(n-i)!}$. That is, $(x + y)^n = \binom{n}{0}x^n + \binom{n}{1}x^{n-1}y + \binom{n}{2}x^{n-2}y^2 + \binom{n}{n}y^n$. In this case, where $n = 5$, $x = a$, and $y = 2b$, we have:

$$(a + 2b)^5 = \binom{5}{0}a^5 + \binom{5}{1}a^4(2b) + \binom{5}{2}a^3(2b)^2 + \binom{5}{3}a^2(2b)^3 + \binom{5}{4}a(2b)^4 + \binom{5}{5}(2b)^5$$
$$= (1)a^5 + (5)a^4(2b) + (10)a^3(4b^2) + (10)a^2(8b^3) + (5)a(16b^4) + (1)(32b^5)$$
$$= a^5 + 10a^4b + 40\,a^3b^2 + 80\,a^2b^3 + 80ab^4 + 32b^5$$

The only one of the answer choices that does not appear as a term of this polynomial is D, $40ab^4$.

49. C: The sum of two logarithms of the same base is equal to the logarithm of the product, and the difference of two logarithms of the same base is equal to the logarithm of the quotient. That is, $\log_b x + \log_b y = \log_b(xy)$, and $\log_b x - \log_b y = \log_b \frac{x}{y}$. Therefore, $\ln 7 + \ln 5 - \ln 3 = \ln(7 \times 5) - \ln 3 = \ln 35 - \ln 3 = \ln\frac{35}{3}$.

50. A: $\sec \theta = \frac{1}{\cos \theta}$, or, equivalently, $\cos \theta = \frac{1}{\sec \theta}$. Therefore, if $\sec \theta = 2$, then $\cos \theta = \frac{1}{2}$. $\cos \theta = \frac{1}{2}$ when $\theta = 60°$ or $300°$; $\sin 60° = \frac{\sqrt{3}}{2}$ and $\sin 300° = -\frac{\sqrt{3}}{2}$. Alternatively, use the Pythagorean identity $\sin^2 \theta + \cos^2 \theta = 1$ to find $\sin \theta$, so $\sin^2 \theta = 1 - \cos^2 \theta$, and $\sin \theta = \pm\sqrt{1 - \cos^2 \theta} = \pm\sqrt{1 - \left(\frac{1}{2}\right)^2} = \pm\sqrt{1 - \frac{1}{4}} = \pm\sqrt{\frac{3}{4}} = \pm\frac{\sqrt{3}}{2}$. (Whether the sine is positive or negative depends on what quadrant the angle is in; there is not enough information given in the problem to determine that, which is why the problem only asks which of the answer choices is a *possible* value for $\sin \theta$.)

51. C: The five choices all have the two lines that mark the boundaries of the inequalities plotted identically; the only difference is which sides are shaded. It's therefore not necessary to check that the lines are correct; simply determine which of the areas bounded by the lines pertain to the

system of inequalities. One way to do that is to pick a point in each region and check whether it satisfies the inequalities. For instance, in the region on the left, we can pick the origin, $(0, 0)$. Since $0 - 0 \not> 1$ and $2(0) + 0 \not> 2$, this does not satisfy either inequality. From the top region we can choose, for example, the point $(0, 3)$. $0 - 3 \not> 1$, so this fails to satisfy the first inequality. From the bottom region we can choose, for instance, $(0, -2)$. $0 - (-2) > 1$, so the first inequality is satisfied, but $2(0) + (-2) \not> 2$, so the second is not. Finally, from the rightmost region we can choose, for example, the point $(2, 0)$. $2 - 0 > 1$ and $2(2) + 0 > 2$, so both inequalities are satisfied; this is the only region that should be shaded in.

52. E: $f\big(g(x)\big) = f\left(x + \frac{3}{2}\right) = 2\left(x + \frac{3}{2}\right) - 3 = 2x + 2 \times \frac{3}{2} - 3 = 2x + 3 - 3 = 2x$. So the statement that $f\big(g(z)\big) = 6$ is equivalent to $2z = 6$. Dividing both sides of this equation by 2, we find $z = 3$.

53. A: The numbers $1, \frac{2}{3}, \frac{4}{9}, \frac{8}{27}, \ldots$ form a geometric sequence, since the ratio of any two consecutive terms is the same, namely $\frac{2}{3}$. What the problem is asking for, then, is the sum of an infinite geometric sequence. This sum exists (and is finite) whenever the absolute value of the common ratio r is less than one; since $\left|\frac{2}{3}\right| < 1$, that condition is satisfied. The formula for the sum of an infinite geometric series is $S_\infty = \frac{a_1}{1-r}$, where a_1 is the first term of the series and r is the common ratio; putting in the appropriate values of $a_1 = 1$ and $r = \frac{2}{3}$, we get $S_\infty = \frac{1}{1-\frac{2}{3}} = \frac{1}{\frac{1}{3}} = 3$.

54. A: A square matrix A is invertible—that is, there exists another matrix A^{-1} such that $A A^{-1} = A^{-1}A = I$, where I is the identity matrix, $\begin{bmatrix} 1 & 0 \\ 0 & 1 \end{bmatrix}$ (or its higher-order version)—if and only if its *determinant* is nonzero. For a 2×2 matrix $\begin{bmatrix} a & b \\ c & d \end{bmatrix}$ like the ones given in the answer choices, the determinant is $ad - bc$. The determinant of the matrix in choice A is $1 \times 6 - 2 \times 3 = 6 - 6 = 0$, so that matrix is not invertible. The determinants of the matrices in the other four choices are -6, -16, -9, and 9, respectively: since these determinants are all nonzero, the four matrices in choices B, C, D, and E are all invertible.

55. D: To determine the probability of Susan's drawing two left and two right socks from the drawer, we can determine the total number of possible sets of two left socks and two right socks, and divide by the total number of possible sets of four socks. If there are eight pairs of socks in the drawer, then there are eight left socks, so the total number of possible sets of two left socks that can be drawn is $_8C_2 = \binom{8}{2} = \frac{8!}{2!(8-2)!} = \frac{8 \times 7 \times 6!}{2! \times 6!} = \frac{56}{2} = 28$. By the same logic, there are also 28 possible sets of two right socks that can be drawn. Since there are 16 socks in the drawer in all, the total number of possible sets of four socks that can be drawn is $_{16}C_4 = \binom{16}{4} = \frac{16!}{4!(16-4)!} = \frac{16 \times 15 \times 14 \times 13 \times 12!}{4! \times 12!} = \frac{16 \times 15 \times 14 \times 13}{4 \times 3 \times 2 \times 1}$

$= 4 \times 5 \times 7 \times 13 = 1820$. The probability of her drawing two left socks and two right socks is therefore $\frac{28 \times 28}{1820} = \frac{28}{65}$.

56. E: We can write the quotient as a fraction: $\frac{2+\sqrt{3}}{2-\sqrt{3}}$. Now, we need to *rationalize the denominator* -- that is, to convert this fraction to a form without any radicals in the denominator. To do this, we multiply both sides of the fraction by the conjugate of the denominator: $\frac{(2+\sqrt{3})\times(2+\sqrt{3})}{(2-\sqrt{3})\times(2+\sqrt{3})}$. We can

- 38 -

simplify both the numerator and the denominator by using the FOIL method, for First, Inner, Outer, Last:

$$\left(2 + \sqrt{3}\right) \times \left(2 + \sqrt{3}\right) = 2 \times 2 + 2 \times \sqrt{3} + \sqrt{3} \times 2 + \sqrt{3} \times \sqrt{3} = 4 + 2\sqrt{3} + 2\sqrt{3} + 3 = 7 + 4\sqrt{3}$$
$$\left(2 - \sqrt{3}\right) \times \left(2 + \sqrt{3}\right) = 2 \times 2 + 2 \times \sqrt{3} + \left(-\sqrt{3}\right) \times 2 + \left(-\sqrt{3}\right) \times \sqrt{3} = 4 + 2\sqrt{3} - 2\sqrt{3} - 3 = 1$$

The fraction then becomes $\frac{7+4\sqrt{3}}{1}$, or simply $7 + 4\sqrt{3}$.

57. E: The half-life of an isotope is the amount of time it takes for it to decay to half its former amount. 8,000 years is five times the half-life of 1,600 years, so the amount of ^{226}Ra would have been halved five times. That is, the original amount would have been multiplied by $\left(\frac{1}{2}\right)^5 = \frac{1}{32}$. So if we call the original amount of ^{226}Ra x, then we know $\frac{1}{32}x = 2$ g, so $x = 2$ g $\times 32 = 64$ g.

58. D: Any diameter of a circle must pass through its center, and, conversely, any line through the center of a circle includes a diameter of the circle. The question, then, is equivalent to asking which of the given lines passes through the center of the circle. The standard form of the equation of a circle is $(x - h)^2 + (y - k)^2 = r^2$, where r is the circle's radius and (h, k) is its center. In the case of the given equation, $(x - 1)^2 + (y - 2)^2 = 4$, $h = 1$ and $k = 2$, so the center of the circle is the point $(1, 2)$. The simplest way to check which line passes through the point $(1, 2)$ is just to substitute $x = 1$ and $y = 2$ into the equation of each line and see which equation remains true. Since $2 \neq 1 - \frac{1}{2}$, $2 \neq 2 \times 1 + 2$, $2 \neq 2 \times 1 + 4$, and $2 \neq 4 \times 1 + 2$, the lines in choices A, B, C, and E do not pass through the point $(1, 2)$. However, $2 = 3 \times 1 - 1$, so the equation of line D is satisfied.

59. B: From the given information, we can sketch the following figure (not to scale):

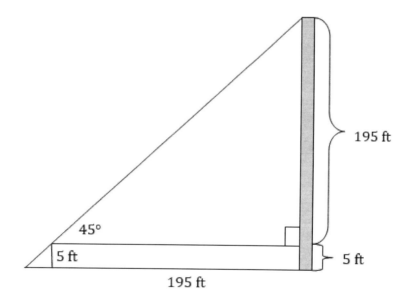

The legs of a 45°-45°-90° triangle are congruent; therefore, the vertical distance from the top of the tower to Sylvia's horizontal line of sight is the same as the distance Sylvia stands from the tower, 195 feet. Since Sylvia is approximately 5 feet tall, the height of the tower is approximately 195 ft + 5 ft = 200 ft.

60. C: By the relation of logarithms to exponents, if $p^q = r$ then $q = \log_p r$. This, however, is not one of the answer choices. (Choice E is $\log_r p$, but this reverses the p and the r and is not the same thing.) However, we can use the change of base formula, $\log_x y = \frac{\log_b y}{\log_b x}$ for any positive base B. In particular, we can choose $b = e$, the base of the natural logarithm, so $\log_p r = \frac{\log_e r}{\log_e p} = \frac{\ln r}{\ln p}$.

Practice Test #2

Reading

*[The Time Traveller is talking to his friends. He has just explained that while three dimensions—
length, breadth, and thickness — are typically accepted, a "fourth dimension" should also be
considered.]*

'Well, I do not mind telling you I have been at work upon this geometry of Four Dimensions for
some time. Some of my results are curious. For instance, here is a portrait of a man at eight years
old, another at fifteen, another at seventeen, another at twenty-three, and so on. All these are
evidently sections, as it were, Three-Dimensional representations of his Four-Dimensioned being,
which is a fixed and unalterable thing.

'Scientific people,' proceeded the Time Traveller, after the pause required for the proper
assimilation of this, 'know very well that Time is only a kind of Space. Here is a popular scientific
diagram, a weather record. This line I trace with my finger shows the movement of the barometer.
Yesterday it was so high, yesterday night it fell, then this morning it rose again, and so gently
upward to here. Surely the mercury did not trace this line in any of the dimensions of Space
generally recognized? But certainly it traced such a line, and that line, therefore, we must conclude
was along the Time-Dimension.'

'But,' said the Medical Man, staring hard at a coal in the fire, 'if Time is really only a fourth
dimension of Space, why is it, and why has it always been, regarded as something different? And
why cannot we move in Time as we move about in the other dimensions of Space?'

The Time Traveller smiled. 'Are you sure we can move freely in Space? Right and left we can go,
backward and forward freely enough, and men always have done so. I admit we move freely in two
dimensions. But how about up and down? Gravitation limits us there.'

'Not exactly,' said the Medical Man. 'There are balloons.'

'But before the balloons, save for spasmodic jumping and the inequalities of the surface, man
had no freedom of vertical movement.'

'Still they could move a little up and down,' said the Medical Man.

'Easier, far easier down than up.'

'And you cannot move at all in Time, you cannot get away from the present moment.'

'My dear sir, that is just where you are wrong. That is just where the whole world has gone
wrong..."

[Adapted from H. G. Wells, *The Time Machine* (1895)]

1. Which of the following best summarizes the above selection?
    a. It is a conversation involving the age of men and space.
    b. It is a conversation about the nature of time and space.
    c. It is a dialogue from two friends about their medical ideas.
    d. It is a dialogue from two colleagues about time and distance.

2. As referred to in paragraph 6 above, what is a synonym for the word "spasmodic"?
   a. Required
   b. Impromptu
   c. Occasional
   d. Surprising

3. What effect does the point-of-view in this story have on its development?
   a. It makes the reader feel intelligent.
   b. It creates confusion.
   c. It builds suspense.
   d. It develops a feeling of contentment.

4. How can you tell that the men's regular work is important?
   a. The author does not identify them by name, but by occupation.
   b. The author mentions the free movement of an object in space.
   c. The author mentions portraits of an aging person.
   d. None of the above

Passage One

Four score and seven years ago our fathers brought forth, upon this continent, a new nation, conceived in Liberty, and dedicated to the proposition that all men are created equal.

Now we are engaged in a great civil war, testing whether that nation, or any nation so conceived, and so dedicated, can long endure. We are met here on a great battlefield of that war. We have come to dedicate a portion of it as a final resting place for those who here gave their lives that that nation might live. It is altogether fitting and proper that we should do this.

But in a larger sense we cannot dedicate - we cannot consecrate - we cannot hallow this ground. The brave men, living and dead, who struggled here, have consecrated it far above our poor power to add or detract. The world will little note, nor long remember, what we say here, but can never forget what they did here.

It is for us, the living, rather to be dedicated here to the unfinished work which they have, thus far, so nobly carried on. It is rather for us to be here dedicated to the great task remaining before us - that from these honored dead we take increased devotion to that cause for which they here gave the last full measure of devotion - that we here highly resolve that these dead shall not have died in vain; that this nation shall have a new birth of freedom; and that this government of the people, by the people, for the people, shall not perish from the earth.

[From Abraham Lincoln, "The Gettysburg Address" (1863)]

Passage Two

Let us not wallow in the valley of despair, I say to you today, my friends.

And so even though we face the difficulties of today and tomorrow, I still have a dream. It is a dream deeply rooted in the American dream.

I have a dream that one day this nation will rise up and live out the true meaning of its creed: "We hold these truths to be self-evident, that all men are created equal."

I have a dream that one day on the red hills of Georgia, the sons of former slaves and the sons of former slave owners will be able to sit down together at the table of brotherhood.

I have a dream that one day even the state of Mississippi, a state sweltering with the heat of injustice, sweltering with the heat of oppression, will be transformed into an oasis of freedom and justice.

I have a dream that my four little children will one day live in a nation where they will not be judged by the color of their skin but by the content of their character.

I have a dream today!

[Adapted from Martin Luther King Jr., "I Have a Dream" (1963)]

5. What is the main message of Passage One?
   a. Those who died in this battle honor this land we are dedicating today better than anyone else.
   b. As we honor those who died in this battle, we should move forward with renewed dedication to ensuring the nation our founding fathers created continues to function the way they intended.
   c. We need to put the regrets of the past aside, without remembering the sacrifices of those who gave their lives for our country.
   d. The war we are fighting is far from over, as evidenced by the number of lives lost in this battle.

6. In the first passage, there were nearly 100 years between the American Revolution and the Civil War. The speech connects ideas about these two conflicts by saying that the ideas of the Civil War
   a. threaten those of the Revolution.
   b. are similar to those of the Revolution.
   c. are newer than those of the Revolution.
   d. are better than those of the Revolution.

7. How do the authors use time in their respective speeches?
   a. Lincoln talks about the present before he talks about the past, and King addresses the hope of the future
   b. Lincoln addresses the present, and King talks about the past before he talks about the present
   c. Lincoln addresses the hope of the future, and King talks about the present before he talks about the past
   d. Lincoln talks about the past before he talks about the present, and King addresses the hope of the future

8. What might be the purpose of Passage Two?
   a. Instructive: To create a more positive feeling about the future of the constitution
   b. Social: To make the audience think about their own dreams and desires
   c. Commercial: To illustrate how unfair the system in Mississippi and Georgia is
   d. Political: To show how things appear to be now and what he hopes will happen

On April 30, 1803, the United States bought the Louisiana Territory from the French. Astounded and excited by the offer of a sale and all that it would mean, it took less than a month to hear the offer and determine to buy it for $15 million. Right away the United States had more than twice the amount of land as before, giving the country more of a chance to become powerful. They had to move in military and governmental power in this region, but even as this was happening they had very little knowledge about the area. They did not even really know where the land boundaries were, nor did they have any idea how many people lived there. They needed to explore.

9. Based on the facts in the passage, what prediction could you make about the time immediately following the Louisiana Purchase?

    a. Explorers were already on the way to the region.
    b. The government wanted to become powerful.
    c. People in government would make sure explorers went to the region.
    d. Explorers would want to be paid for their work.

It was the best of times, it was the worst of times, it was the age of wisdom, it was the age of foolishness, it was the epoch of belief, it was the epoch of incredulity, it was the season of Light, it was the season of Darkness, it was the spring of hope, it was the winter of despair, we had everything before us, we had nothing before us, we were all going direct to heaven, we were all going direct the other way – in short, the period was so far like the present period, that some of its noisiest authorities insisted on its being received, for good or for evil, in the superlative degree of comparison only.

[Adapted from Charles Dickens *A Tale of Two Cities* (1859)]

10. Which best expresses one main idea that Dickens wanted readers to realize from this introduction?

    a. That everything could seem to be best or worst according to individual perceptions
    b. That the past described was so identical to the present they were indistinguishable
    c. That the past and present both had equal balances of good/light and evil/darkness
    d. That the extremities of good and bad described were imagined by the "authorities"

Adelaide: Mainstream cleaning supplies are dangerous for people, because they contain toxic chemicals such as phosphates. Young children are especially at risk for asthma and other diseases from these airborne chemicals, plus some of the cleaning products can imitate estrogen and cause severe health problems for women. Natural cleaning products are safe and effective, however, so people should consider switching to healthier and more environmentally friendly cleaning alternatives.

Marcel: But natural cleaning products are not as strong as the mainstream products and often fail to provide the same level of cleanliness. If parents keep the cleaning products out of reach, the products will not create a serious risk for children. And the mainstream cleaning products are cheaper and thus more economical for families to purchase.

11. Marcel responded to Adelaide's argument by doing which of the following?

    a. Ignoring the main point that Adelaide is making and redirecting his focus to different topics
    b. Ceding the main point of Adelaide's argument but suggesting a problem that Adelaide fails to address
    c. Relying on apocryphal and unsupported information to formulate a separate argument
    d. Overlooking important details of Adelaide's argument and thus failing to counter her claims with sufficient objection

The following statements were made by several of your classmates in a discussion on providing universal government health care.

> Abner: We need the government to step in and manage health care because hospital bills are too expensive.

> Mauri: Government health care would mean that politicians now control what care and medicines you have access to.

> Ping: Insurance companies deny too many people coverage. Government health care sounds like it would be good because everyone gets insurance. But then you just have the government denying care.

12. Which of the following choices synthesizes the ideas and draws a conclusion?

a. This debate is about health care. It seems that we need the government to help manage the rising costs of health care so everyone has access. We also need to deal with the unfair practices of insurance companies. If the government manages health care, everyone will be covered and be able to go to the hospital whenever they are sick.

b. According to the debate so far, rising hospital costs and insurance problems are good reasons to get the government involved in health care. However, the government will then control a big part of your life and can deny certain treatments. It seems like there are many pros and cons here: we must decide what we want to give up: some of our access to health care or some of our liberties.

c. According to the speakers here, the government control of health care is full of downsides. No one wants to pay a lot of money for health care, but that's only one problem. When the government manages something, it all comes down to politicians controlling what you can and can't have or do. What happens when politicians decide they won't cover expensive treatments for your dying mother? Or what if they decide everyone must eat broccoli?

d. It seems that there are different points of view here. If the government controls health care, it might affect the rising costs. Everyone would have access to health care. However, politicians would control all aspects of health care, too. Insurance companies are not allowing people to get coverage. However, the government may decide that people should not have certain medicines.

I had swooned; but still will not say that all of consciousness was lost. What of it there remained I will not attempt to define, or even to describe; yet all was not lost. In the deepest slumber—no! In delirium—no! In a swoon—no! In death—no! Even in the grave all was not lost. Else there is no immortality for man. Arousing from the most profound of slumbers, we break the gossamer web of some dream. Yet in a second afterwards (so frail may that web have been) we remember not that we have dreamed. In the return to life from the swoon there are two stages; first, that of the sense of mental or spiritual; secondly, that of the sense of physical existence.

[Adapted from Edgar Allan Poe, "The Pit and the Pendulum" (1843)]

13. The selection is written in
   a. First-person narration
   b. Third-person narration
   c. First-person omniscient narration
   d. Epistolary narrative voice

Two years before the idea of digging at Panama had been thought of, the ground where the Nicaragua Canal is being built had been surveyed, and thought better suited to the purpose than Panama.

The reason for this was, that at Panama a long and deep cut had to be made through the mountains. This had to be done by blasting, in much the same way that the rocks are cleared away to build houses. This is a long and tedious work.

The Nicaragua Canal will be 159 miles long, while the Panama, if it is ever completed, will be only 59 miles; but of these 159 miles, 117 are through the Nicaragua Lake and the San Juan River—water-ways already made by nature. For the remaining distance, there are other river-beds that will be used, and only 21 miles will actually have to be cut through.

[Adapted from William B. Harison, *The Great Round World and What is Going On In It* (1896)]

14. What is the tone of this passage?
    a. Informational
    b. Humorous
    c. Mysterious
    d. Angry

In the United States, the foreign language requirement for high school graduation is decided at the state level. This means the requirement varies, with some states deciding to forego a foreign language requirement altogether (www.ncssfl.org). It is necessary that these states reconsider their position and amend their requirements to reflect compulsory completion of a course of one or more foreign languages. Studying a foreign language has become increasingly important for the global economy. As technology continues to make international business relations increasingly easy, people need to keep up by increasing their communication capabilities. High school graduates with foreign language credits have been shown to have an increased college acceptance rate. In addition, students who have mastered more than one language typically find themselves in greater demand when they reach the job market. Students who did not study a foreign language often find themselves unable to obtain a job at all.

15. Which of the following statements represents the best summary of the claims made in this passage?
    a. Studying a foreign language is important if you want to graduate from high school and get a job.
    b. Studying a foreign language is important for the global economy because of the technological advances that have been made in international communications.
    c. Studying a foreign language is important for the global economy, college acceptance rates, and becoming a sought-after candidate in the job market.
    d. Studying a foreign language is important for college acceptance rates and obtaining a job after college.

Harriet Tubman was a runaway slave from Maryland who became known as the "Moses of her people." Over the course of 10 years, and at great personal risk, she led hundreds of slaves to freedom along the Underground Railroad, a secret network of safe houses where runaway slaves could stay on their journey north to freedom. She later became a leader in the abolitionist movement, and during the Civil War she was a spy for the federal forces in South Carolina as well as a nurse.

Harriet Tubman's name at birth was Araminta Ross. She was one of 11 children of Harriet and Benjamin Ross born into slavery in Dorchester County, Maryland. As a child, Ross was "hired out" by her master as a nursemaid for a small baby. Ross had to stay awake all night so that the baby wouldn't cry and wake the mother. If Ross fell asleep, the baby's mother whipped her. From a very young age, Ross was determined to gain her freedom.

16. How is this passage structured?
    a. cause and effect
    b. problem and solution
    c. chronological order
    d. compare and contrast

The road to wealth is, as Dr. Franklin truly says, "as plain as the road to the mill." It consists simply in expending less than we earn; that seems to be a very simple problem. Mr. Micawber, one of those happy creations of the genial Dickens, puts the case in a strong light when he says that to have annual income of twenty pounds per annum, and spend twenty pounds and sixpence, is to be the most miserable of men; whereas, to have an income of only twenty pounds, and spend but nineteen pounds and sixpence is to be the happiest of mortals.

Many of my readers may say, "we understand this: this is economy, and we know economy is wealth; we know we can't eat our cake and keep it also." Yet I beg to say that perhaps more cases of failure arise from mistakes on this point than almost any other. The fact is, many people think they understand economy when they really do not.

17. What is the best definition of *economy* as it is used in this passage?
    a. exchange of money, goods, and services
    b. delegation of household affairs
    c. efficient money management
    d. less expensive

I was born at Blunderstone, in Suffolk, or 'there by', as they say in Scotland. I was a posthumous child. My father's eyes had closed upon the light of this world six months, when mine opened on it. There is something strange to me, even now, in the reflection that he never saw me; and something stranger yet in the shadowy remembrance that I have of my first childish associations with his white grave-stone in the churchyard, and of the indefinable compassion I used to feel for it lying out alone there in the dark night, when our little parlour was warm and bright with fire and candle, and the doors of our house were—almost cruelly, it seemed to me sometimes—bolted and locked against it.

18. How does the author convey sadness?
    a. Through the discussion of his birth in Scotland half a year after his father had passed away.
    b. Through his description of his memories about his father's grave stone and its location.
    c. Through his reflection in the mirror and his memories about his first explorations into the darkness.
    d. Through his recollection that he had been born six months after his father died, and that his father had never seen his own son.

19. These birds are not _____ to North America; they were brought here by European immigrants.

    a. exigent
    b. fluent
    c. indigenous
    d. ingenuous

20. I want to _____ a change in the program, so I will have to present a solution that will have a strong _____ on the board.

    a. affect, affect
    b. affect, effect
    c. effect, effect
    d. effect, affect

Writing

(1) After Orville and Wilbur Wright have flown their first airplane in 1903, the age of flying slowly began. (2) Many new pilots learned how to fly in World War I, which the United States joined in 1917. (3) During the war, the American public loved hearing stories about the daring pilots and their air fights. (4) But after the war ended, many Americans thought that men and women belonged on the ground and not in the air.

(5) In the years after the war and through the Roaring Twenties, America's pilots found themselves without jobs. (6) Some of them gave up flying altogether. (7) Pilot Eddie Rickenbacker, who used to be called America's Ace of Aces, became a car salesman. (8) But other pilots found new and creative things to do with their airplanes.

(9) Pilot Casey Jones used his airplane to help get news across the country. (10) When a big news story broke, Jones flew news photos to newspapers in different cities. (11) Another pilot, Roscoe Turner traveled around the country with a lion cub in his plane. (12) The cub was the mascot of an oil company, and Turner convinced the company that flying the cub around would be a good advertisement. (13) The Humane Society wasn't very happy about this idea, and they convinced Turner to make sure the lion cub always wore a parachute.

(14) During the 1920s, the U.S. Post Office developed airmail. (15) Before airmail, the post traveled on trains and can take weeks to reach a destination. (16) Flying for the post office was dangerous work. (17) Early pilots didn't have sophisticated instruments and safety equipment on their planes. (18) Many of them had to bail out and use their parachutes when their planes iced up in the cold air or had other trouble.

1. What change should be made to sentence 1?
   a. Add a comma after *Wright*
   b. Change *have flown* to *flew*
   c. Change *first* to *1st*
   d. Delete the comma after *1903*

2. What is the best way to combine sentences 5 and 6?
   a. Some of America's pilots in the years after the war and through the Roaring Twenties found themselves without jobs because they gave up flying altogether.
   b. In the years after the war and through the Roaring Twenties, America's pilots found themselves without jobs; thus some of them gave up flying altogether.
   c. Some of America's pilots gave up flying altogether in the years after the war and through the Roaring Twenties, and they found themselves without jobs.
   d. In the years after the war and through the Roaring Twenties, America's pilots found themselves without jobs because some of them gave up flying altogether.

3. What change should be made in sentence 11?
   a. Delete the comma before *Roscoe*
   b. Add a comma after *Turner*
   c. Change *with* to *as*
   d. Change *plane* to *airplane*

4. What change should be made to sentence 15?

    a. Delete the comma after *airmail*
    b. Change *traveled* to *travelled*
    c. Change *can* to *could*
    d. Change *a* to *it's*

5. What is the best way to combine sentences 15 and 16?

    a. Flying for the post office was dangerous work, but early pilots didn't have sophisticated instruments and safety equipment on their planes.
    b. Early pilots didn't have sophisticated instruments and safety equipment on their planes which made flying for the post office dangerous work.
    c. Flying for the post office was dangerous work; however, early pilots didn't have sophisticated instruments and safety equipment on their planes.
    d. Early pilots didn't have sophisticated instruments and safety equipment on their planes, nor was flying for the post office dangerous work.

(1) Sparky was a loser, but he didn't stay that way. (2) You probably know Sparky better by his given name: Charles Schulz. (3) Nicknamed Sparky when he was a child, Charles schulz endured years of struggle before he finally found success. (4) Eventually, the loser became a winner. (5) Thanks to the hard work and perseverance of Sparky, the world will always remember a boy named Charlie Brown and the rest of the Peanuts gang.

(6) Sparky was born Charles Monroe Schulz on November 26, 1922, and he grew up in Minneapolis, Minnesota, where he struggled to fit in socially. (7) He skipped two grades, and as a result he struggled with his studies. (8) He was also painfully shy, so he never dated. (9) In addition, Sparky was inert at most sports. (10) But he loved to draw, drawing was his dream.

(11) Sparky poured his heart and soul into his drawings during his high school years. (12) He had a particular love for cartooning, and he unsuccessfully submitted several cartoons to his yearbook. (13) In the late 1940s, when Sparky was in his mid-twenties, his dream began to come true. (14) Although he was devastated when the cartoons were rejected by the yearbook committee, he remained determined to make a living through his art someday. (15) He sold some cartoons to magazines and newspapers. (16) Someone finally appreciated his artistic ability.

(17) In 1950, Sparky created what would become his legacy; a comic called Peanuts. (18) The central character—Charlie Brown—was based on Sparky himself, and his lifelong struggle to fit in with the world around him. (19) Peanuts became an instant hit. (20) Adults and children alike were drawn to it because they could relate to the struggles of the characters.

(21) From its humble beginnings in the 1950s, Peanuts went on to become one of the most successful comics of all time. (22) Sparky lovingly hand-drew each of the 18,000 Peanuts comic strips, and they eventually appointed in over 2000 newspapers in more than 75 countries.

6. Which of the following is the most appropriate correction for sentence 3?

    a. Change Sparky to sparky
    b. Change Nicknamed to Nick-named
    c. Remove the comma after child
    d. Change Charles schulz to Charles Schulz

7. Which sentence in paragraph 1 functions as the thesis statement for this composition?

    a. Sentence 2
    b. Sentence 5
    c. Sentence 3
    d. Sentence 1

8. What change, if any, should be made in sentence 10?

    a. No change is necessary
    b. Remove the comma
    c. Replace the comma with a semicolon
    d. Replace the comma with a colon

9. How does sentence 21 function as a transition between paragraph 4 and paragraph 5?

    a. Sentence 21 does not function as a transition
    b. It talks about a topic previously mentioned
    c. It demonstrates transition with the phrase "went on"
    d. It connects the history of Peanuts with the success of Sparky

10. In sentence 22, what word would be most appropriate to replace the misused word "appointed"?

    a. Approximated
    b. Appeared
    c. Appropriated
    d. Appositioned

(1) Some people believe that a student's grades effect whether or not she is a good driver. (2) They want to pass a law that says that teens must have at least a C average in order to get a license to drive. (3) Its true that many students who do all of their work and work hard will get at least a C or higher, but there are many factors that go into getting good grades. (4) Therefore, I believe this law is unfair and shouldn't be passed.

(5) In some classes, like math, there are clear right or wrong answers. (6) If I say 3+2=6, then I should lose a point. (7) However, grading can be very subjective and may depend on the teacher's opinion rather than facts. (8) For example when I am graded for this essay, my teacher will have to use her opinion to determine its quality. (9) If I do something my teacher doesn't like but isn't necessarily wrong, I could still get a bad grade.

(10) Furthermore, it's not always possible to know a teacher's expectations. I had a teacher who took over a month to return written assignments. (11) This meant that I often made the same mistake over and over again and constantly got lower grades. (12) I never had the opportunity to learn from my mistakes because I didn't get enough feedback, but this was not my fault. (13) I shouldn't loose my chance to get a driver's license because my teacher does not give good and timely feedback.

(14) Instead of looking at a student's grades to decide weather or not to give a license, the state should look at driving ability. (15) Lawmakers who are concerned about the quality of student drivers can pass laws requiring more training or creating a harder driving test. (16) However, they should not require students to maintain a certain grade point average. (17) It doesn't have any bearing on driving ability and should not be considered.

11. What change should be made to sentence 3?

    a. Change *Its* to *It's*
    b. Change *who* to *whom*
    c. Change *their* to *they're*
    d. Delete the comma after *higher*

12. What transition word or phrase, if any, should replace *furthermore* in sentence 10?

    a. Therefore
    b. Instead
    c. For that reason
    d. No change

13. Which choice best divides sentence 12 into two shorter sentences?

    a. I never had the opportunity to learn from my mistakes. Because I didn't get enough feedback, but this was not my fault.
    b. I never had the opportunity to learn from mistakes. I didn't get enough feedback because this was not my fault.
    c. I never had the opportunity to learn from my mistakes. I didn't get enough feedback, but this was not my fault.
    d. Because I never had the opportunity to learn from my mistakes, I didn't get enough feedback. This was not my fault.

14. What change should be made to sentence 13?

    a. Change *loose* to *lose.*
    b. Change *driver's* to *drivers.*
    c. Insert a comma after *license.*
    d. Insert a comma after *good.*

15. What is the most effective way, if any, to rewrite sentence 15?

    a. If lawmakers are concerned about the quality of student drivers, they can pass laws requiring more training or a harder driving test.
    b. If lawmakers are concerned, they can pass laws about the quality of student drivers; requiring more training or a harder driving test.
    c. Concerned about the quality of student drivers, lawmakers can pass laws requiring more training or a harder driving test.
    d. No change.

(1) The Freedom Trail is in Boston, Massachusetts and it's a two and a half mile path through the center of Boston that takes you past buildings and places that were important in Boston's history and in Revolutionary War history.

(2) The trail begins on the Boston Common, which is a big park with baseball fields and large grassy stretches. (3) Back in 1634 when it was first established, the Boston Common was usually used to keep livestock like cows. (4) Later, it was a place where soldiers camped out when they passed through the city.

(5) A bit down from the Boston Common is the New State House, which was built in 1798, over 150 years after the Boston Common. (6) Paul Revere helped to decorate the State House by laying copper over the wood. (7) The Old State House, which gave its name to the new one, is located a few blocks away.

(8) The Granary Burying Ground is another spot on the Freedom Trail and is famous because many revolutionary figures are buried in it. (9) The Granary was first used as a cemetery in 1660 and got its name because it was next to a grain storage building. (10) The burying ground has 2,345 markers or gravestones, but some people think that up to 8,000 people are buried in it. (11) Some of the most famous people resting at the Granary are Benjamin Franklin's parents, John Hancock, Paul Revere, and victims of the Boston Massacre.

(12) The last stop on the Freedom Trail is the USS Constitution, which is a warship that was called Old Ironsides during the War of 1812. (13) Paul Revere had his hand in this ship as well because he created the copper fastenings on the ship. (14) These are just a few of the stops on the Freedom Trail which is a great way for families to learn about the Revolutionary War and colonial times together. (15) Visit the Freedom Trail if you literally want to walk through history!

16. Which change should be made to sentence 1?

    a. Add a comma after *Massachusetts*
    b. Change *it's* to *its*
    c. Add a comma after *buildings*
    d. Add a comma after *Boston's history*

17. What change should be made to sentence 3?

    a. Change 1634 to sixteen-thirty-four
    b. Add a comma after 1634
    c. Change first to 1st
    d. Change usually to unusually

The following is sentence 6: *Paul Revere helped to decorate the State House by laying copper over the wood.*

The writer is considering adding the following after Paul Revere: *who was the first American to find success with rolling copper into sheets for use as sheathing,*

18. Should the author add this piece to the passage?

    a. Yes, this is evidence for Paul Revere being regarded as famous.
    b. No, this draws attention away from the focus of the passage.
    c. Yes, this is interesting information that readers will appreciate.
    d. No, this sentence is an opinion of the author.

19. What's the most effective way to revise sentence 7?

    a. Because there is an Old State House a few blocks away, the New State House got its name
    b. The Old State House, located a few blocks away, got its name from the New State House
    c. A few blocks away from the New State House is the Old State House, which lent its name to the new State House
    d. The New State House got its name because there is an Old State House a few blocks away

20. What's the most effective way, if any, to revise sentence 11?

    a. Resting at the Granary are some of the most famous people like Benjamin Franklin's parents, John Hancock, Paul Revere, and victims of the Boston Massacre.
    b. Benjamin Franklin's parents, John Hancock, Paul Revere, and victims of the Boston Massacre are resting at the Granary, which has some of the most famous people.
    c. Some of the most famous people, like Benjamin Franklin's parents, John Hancock, Paul Revere, and victims of the Boston Massacre are resting at the Granary.
    d. No change.

(1) Dear Mrs. Alloway and the Board,

(2) At the school board meeting on January 25, you passed a rule banning soft drinks from the school cafeteria as of the beginning of the next school year. (3) While I agree with your assessment that soft drinks consumed in access can be detrimental to the health of students and adults, I do not agree with the decision to make them unavailable to the student body.

(4) Soft drinks have a significant amount of sugar and can be unhealthy when drunk in large quantities. (5) My classmates and I realize this, but a soft drink is no less unhealthy than many of the food that will continue to be served in the cafeteria. (6) For example, the average 12 ounce soft drink has about 150 calories, no fat, and 39 grams of sugar. (7) The cookies that will continue to be served in the cafeteria (and that were served at the school board meeting) have approximately 190 calories, 9 grams of fat, and 14 grams of sugar. (8) Honestly, it's dumb that soft drinks are being discriminated against. (9) If the school board is serious about promoting healthy eating in the school cafeteria all items served should meet nutritional requirements, not just drinks.

(10) Furthermore, my peers and I are all adolescents and preparing for adulthood. (11) Some of us will be heading off to college in just a year or two and will be living independently. (12) Banning soft drinks in the high school could potentially cause us to drink even more soft drinks when we are not in the high school. (13) Instead, I propose that the school board educate students about making smart choices. (14) By allowing soft drinks in the high school, the school board can ensure that my peers and I learn how to eat and drink responsibly, making us healthier for the rest of our lives.

(15) Instead of banning soft drinks, I propose that the school cafeteria charge higher prices for items that do not meet certain nutritional standards: including those chocolate chip cookies. (16) The extra money brought in can be used to educate students about healthy eating choices. (17) The higher prices may encourage students to naturally make healthier choices. (18) This method will accomplish the school board's goal of getting students to drink fewer soft drinks, but will still give the students choice and the respect that they deserve.

Sincerely,

Elyse Chan

Student Congress President

21. Which of the following sentences should be deleted from the second paragraph in order to maintain the focus of the paragraph?

    a. Sentence 4
    b. Sentence 5
    c. Sentence 7
    d. Sentence 8

22. Which word could be deleted from sentence 12 without changing the meaning of the sentence?

  a. Soft, as it used after *banning*
  b. Potentially
  c. Us
  d. Not

23. Which sentence could best follow and support sentence 13?

  a. Drinking soft drinks is very bad for you
  b. Education will prepare us for college and for living independently
  c. I strongly disagree that the school board should ban soft drinks
  d. It's not fair that no student representatives were invited to the school board meeting

24. What change should be made to sentence 15?

  a. Delete the comma after *drinks*
  b. Change *higher* to *high*
  c. Change *nutritional* to *nutrition*
  d. Delete the colon after standards and put *including those chocolate chip cookies* in parentheses

25. What transition word should be added to the beginning of sentence 17?

  a. Furthermore
  b. However
  c. Although
  d. In conclusion

Mathematics

Arithmetic

Solve the following problems and select your answer from the choices given. You may use the paper you have been given for scratch paper.

1. $4\frac{1}{5} - 2\frac{1}{3} =$

    a. $1\frac{13}{15}$

    b. $2\frac{1}{4}$

    c. $2\frac{2}{15}$

    d. $4\frac{1}{2}$

2. $(2.2 \times 10^3) \times (3.5 \times 10^{-2}) =$

    a. 7.7×10^{-6}

    b. 7.7×10^1

    c. 7.7×10^5

    d. 7.7×10^6

3. What is the proper ordering (from least to greatest) of the following numbers?

    I. $\frac{58}{67}$

    II. 0.58

    III. 58%

    IV. 5.8%

    a. I, III, II, IV

    b. III, IV, II, I

    c. I, III, IV, II

    d. IV, I, III, II

4. In the diagram to the right (not to scale), $x = 91°$ and $y = 42°$. What is z?

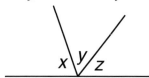

    a. $47°$

    b. $49°$

    c. $66\frac{1}{2}°$

    d. $133°$

5. Doug drives without backtracking from his apartment to a campsite in another state. After two hours, he is halfway to his destination. After four hours, he is two-thirds of the way there. Which of the following could represent the fraction of his travel distance he has covered after three hours?

    a. $\frac{2}{5}$

    b. $\frac{3}{5}$

    c. $\frac{3}{4}$

    d. $\frac{4}{5}$

6. What is 10% of 40%?

    a. 4%
    b. 30%
    c. 50%
    d. 400%

7. $2.62 \times 7.1 =$

    a. 1.462
    b. 14.62
    c. 16.062
    d. 18.602

8. Alan has a large number of cubical building blocks 4 cm on a side. He wants to use them to make a larger solid cube 20 cm on a side. How many building blocks will he need for this?

    a. 25
    b. 94
    c. 125
    d. 150

9. Which of the following inequalities is NOT TRUE?

    a. $\frac{1}{2} > \frac{1}{3} > \frac{1}{4}$

    b. $\frac{1}{5} < \frac{3}{10} < \frac{7}{20}$

    c. $\frac{7}{9} > \frac{2}{3} > \frac{6}{7}$

    d. $\frac{1}{5} < \frac{2}{7} < \frac{3}{10}$

10. Which of the following is closest to $\frac{149}{1502}$?

    a. 0.012
    b. 0.77
    c. 0.103
    d. 0.151

11. Water drains from a bathtub at a rate of one gallon every fifteen seconds. If the bathtub initially has twelve gallons of water in it, how long will it take to drain completely?

    a. 48 seconds
    b. 1 minute 15 seconds
    c. 3 minutes
    d. 4 minutes

12. $\frac{7}{8} \times \frac{2}{3} \times \frac{4}{5} \times \frac{3}{7} =$

    a. $\frac{1}{7}$

    b. $\frac{1}{5}$

    c. $\frac{3}{8}$

    d. 1

13. What is the average of 2.02, 0.275, and 1.98?

    a. 1.1375
    b. 1.375
    c. 1.425
    d. 2.25

14. The following numbers are constants (shown with their three digit approximations) from mathematics and science:

$$\gamma \approx 0.577$$

$$\phi \approx 1.618$$

$$\pi \approx 3.142$$

Which of the following represents the smallest number?

    a. $\gamma + \phi + \pi$
    b. $(\pi - \phi)^\gamma$
    c. ϕ^γ
    d. π^γ

15. What is 60% of $\frac{5}{6}$?

    a. $\frac{1}{2}$

    b. $\frac{3}{4}$

    c. $\frac{5}{12}$

    d. $\frac{25}{36}$

16. A particular map has a scale of 1 inch = 5 miles. On the map, Lost Canyon Road is one foot long. How long is the actual road?

    a. 2.4 miles
    b. 6 miles
    c. 24 miles
    d. 60 miles

17. $3\frac{1}{4} + 2\frac{5}{6} =$

    a. $5\frac{1}{2}$

    b. $5\frac{3}{5}$

    c. $6\frac{1}{12}$

    d. $6\frac{1}{2}$

18. 50 is what percent of 40?

    a. 80

    b. 90

    c. 120

    d. 125

19. Which of the following is largest?

    a. 0.55

    b. 0.500

    c. 0.505

    d. 0.0555

20. All of the following represent the same number EXCEPT

    a. 0.05

    b. $\frac{1}{50}$

    c. 5×10^{-2}

    d. 5%

Quantitative Reasoning, Algebra, and Statistics

Solve the following problems and select your answer from the choices given. You may use the paper you have been given for scratch paper.

21. What is the value of $\frac{2x-2}{x+3}$ when $x = -1$?

    a. 0

    b. 1

    c. 2

    d. -2

22. Suppose Olivia rolls a regular six-sided die 10 times. What is the expected value for the number of fours that she would have gotten after 10 rolls of the die?

    a. $\frac{3}{4}$

    b. $\frac{5}{2}$

    c. $\frac{5}{3}$

    d. $\frac{8}{9}$

23. Which of the following correctly represents the solution to the inequality $x^2 + 2x \geq x + 6$?

a.
```
-4  -3  -2  -1   0   1   2   3   4
```

b.
```
-4  -3  -2  -1   0   1   2   3   4
```

c.
```
-4  -3  -2  -1   0   1   2   3   4
```

d.
```
-4  -3  -2  -1   0   1   2   3   4
```

24. If $\frac{1}{2x} + \frac{1}{x} = \frac{1}{6}$, then $x =$
   a. 2
   b. 4
   c. 9
   d. 12

25. Kyle bats third in the batting order for the Badgers baseball team. The table below shows the number of hits that Kyle had in each of 7 consecutive games played during one week in July.

Day	Monday	Tuesday	Wednesday	Thursday	Friday	Saturday	Sunday
Hits	1	2	3	1	1	4	2

What is the median of the numbers in the distribution shown in the table?

   a. 1
   b. 2
   c. 3
   d. 4

26. A building has a number of floors of equal height, as well as a thirty-foot spire above them all. If the height of each floor in feet is h, and there are n floors in the building, which of the following represents the building's total height in feet?
   a. $n + h + 30$
   b. $nh + 30$
   c. $30n + h$
   d. $30h + n$

27. $x(y - 2) + y(3 - x) =$
   a. $xy + y$
   b. $-2x + 3y$
   c. $2xy - 2x + 3y$
   d. $xy + 3y - x - 2$

28. Which of the following lists of numbers is ordered from least to greatest?

a. $1, \frac{1}{3}, -\frac{1}{4}, \frac{1}{5}$

b. $\frac{1}{5}, -\frac{1}{4}, \frac{1}{3}, 1$

c. $-\frac{1}{4}, 1, \frac{1}{3}, \frac{1}{5}$

d. $-\frac{1}{4}, \frac{1}{5}, \frac{1}{3}, 1$

29. Consider the following graphic showing demographics of a high school with 1219 total students:

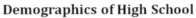

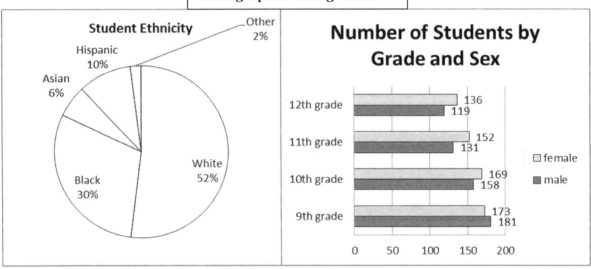

Which of these is the greatest quantity?

    a. The average number of male students in the 11th and 12th grades
    b. The number of Hispanic students at the school
    c. The difference in the number of male and female students at the school
    d. The difference in the number of 9th and 12th grade students at the school

30. In the figure shown, the height of the triangle is three times the height of the square on which it is resting. If the square's width is s, what is the total area taken up by the figure?

   a. $\frac{5}{2}s^2$

   b. $s^2 + \frac{3}{2}s$

   c. $\frac{5}{3}s^2$

   d. $s^2 + 3s$

31. Students at Sunnyside High School participate in football and band. 35% of students play football and play in the band. 42% of students play football. Approximately what percentage of students who play football also march in the band?

   a. 7%

   b. 15%

   c. 23%

   d. 83%

32. $(x + 6)(x - 6) =$

   a. $x^2 - 12x - 36$

   b. $x^2 + 12x - 36$

   c. $x^2 + 12x + 36$

   d. $x^2 - 36$

33. Prizes are to be awarded to the best pupils in each class of an elementary school. The number of students in each grade is shown in the table, and the school principal wants the number of prizes awarded in each grade to be proportional to the number of students. If there are twenty prizes, how many should go to fifth-grade students?

Grade	1	2	3	4	5
Students	35	38	38	33	36

   a. 5

   b. 4

   c. 6

   d. 3

34. If $x + 2y = 3$ and $-x - 3y = 4$, then $x =$

   a. 1

   b. 5

   c. 7

   d. 17

35. Joanie is playing songs on her MP3 player from a 15-song playlist in which every song is equally likely to be played next. Three of the 15 songs are by Beyonce . What is the probability that the next two songs will both be by an artist who is not Beyonce?

  a. 1 in 25
  b. 9 in 25
  c. 16 in 25
  d. 24 in 25

36. At a school carnival, three students spend an average of $10. Six other students spend an average of $4. What is the average amount of money spent by all nine students?

  a. $5
  b. $6
  c. $7
  d. $8

37. Students at Elm and Oak High Schools were surveyed on their favorite type of movies. Given the table below summarizing the responses, which of the following best represents the probability that a student is enrolled at Elm OR prefers Comedies.

	Comedy	Drama	Action	Total
Elm High School	350	225	175	750
Oak High School	325	300	275	900
Total	675	525	450	1650

  a. 45%
  b. 55%
  c. 65%
  d. 75%

38. $-\frac{3}{2}\left(\frac{1}{2}+\frac{1}{3}\right)-\frac{2}{3}\left(\frac{1}{2}-\frac{3}{4}\right) =$

  a. $-1\frac{5}{12}$
  b. $-1\frac{1}{12}$
  c. $-1\frac{1}{2}$
  d. $1\frac{5}{12}$

39. The numbers of volunteers in different states (Texas and New Mexico) for 15 different events are shown in the table below. Which of the following statements best describes the number of volunteers that should be expected at the next event?

TX	12	17	18	19	20	21	21	21	22	28	29	31	41	45	52
NM	7	11	15	28	29	30	31	33	34	36	37	42	44	44	45

a. More volunteers would be expected in New Mexico because it has had more volunteers on 10 of 15 occasions.

b. More volunteers would be expected in Texas because it had the larger maximum number of volunteers.

c. More volunteers would be expected in New Mexico because both the two distributions are reasonably symmetric and New Mexico has a larger median.

d. More volunteers would be expected in Texas because it had a larger mean number of volunteers.

40. How many solutions are there to the equation $|x^2 - 2| = x$?

a. 0

b. 1

c. 2

d. 4

Advanced Algebra and Functions

Solve the following problems and select your answer from the choices given. You may use the paper you have been given for scratch paper.

41. If $\sqrt{2}^2 \cdot 2^{\sqrt{2}} = \left(\sqrt{2}^{\sqrt{2}}\right)^x$, then $x =$

a. 2

b. $\sqrt{2}$

c. $2\sqrt{2}$

d. $2^{\sqrt{2}}$

e. $2 + \sqrt{2}$

42. The interior of what shape is described by the following two inequalities?

$$x^2 + y^2 < 4$$

$$x + y > 3$$

a. A circle

b. A semicircle

c. A circular segment smaller than a semicircle

d. A circular segment larger than a semicircle

e. None; this system of inequalities has no solution.

43. $\dfrac{\ln 81}{\ln 3} =$

    a. 3

    b. $3\sqrt{3}$

    c. 4

    d. ln 3

    e. ln 27

44. Which of the following is a root of $x^2 - 4x + 5$?

    a. 4

    b. $10i$

    c. $1 - i$

    d. $2 + i$

    e. $4 - i$

45. In the triangle, which of the following is equal to $\sin \theta$?

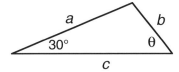

    a. $\dfrac{a}{2b}$

    b. $\dfrac{2b}{a}$

    c. $\dfrac{a}{2c}$

    d. $\dfrac{2a}{c}$

    e. $\dfrac{b}{ac}$

46. If the lines $y = ax + b$ and $y = bx + 2a$ intersect at the point $(2, 3)$, then $a =$

    a. 0

    b. $\dfrac{2}{3}$

    c. 1

    d. $\dfrac{3}{2}$

    e. 3

47. What is the product of three consecutive odd integers, if the one in the middle is x?

    a. $x^2 - 3x$

    b. $x^2 - 5x$

    c. $x^3 - x$

    d. $.x^3 - 4x$

    e. $x^3 + x - 4$

18. $f(x) = ax^b + cx + d$, where a, b, c, and d are all integers. The equation $f(x) = 0$ has exactly one solution, which does *not* occur at a maximum or minimum of $f(x)$. Which of the following *must* be true?

    a. a is positive.
    b. a is negative.
    c. b is odd.
    d. b is even.
    e. c is zero.

49. Six people sit around a circular table at a party. If two of these people are the party's hosts and must sit next to each other, how many different possibilities are there for the order of the six people around the table? (Rotations are not counted as different orders.)

    a. 24
    b. 48
    c. 120
    d. 240
    e. 288

50. Which of the following graphs corresponds to the equation $y = 2\sin(\pi x - \pi)$?

a.
b.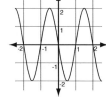

c.
d.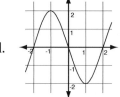

e.

51. If $f(x) = e^{2x}$ and f^{-1} is the inverse of f, then $f\left(f^{-1}(f(x))\right) =$

    a. e^{2x}
    b. $e^{2\ln x}$
    c. $e^{2x}\ln x$
    d. $\ln\left(\frac{1}{2}e^{2x}\right)$
    e. $e^{2\ln\left(\frac{1}{2}e^{2x}\right)}$

52. What geometric shape is defined by the equation $ax + by + cz + d = 0$, where $a, b, c, d \neq 0$?

    a. A point

    b. A line

    c. A plane

    d. A sphere

    e. A hyperboloid

53. $\dfrac{x^7 + 2x^6 + x^5}{x^4 - x^2} =$

    a. $x^3 + 2z$

    b. $x^3 + x + 1$

    c. $\dfrac{x^5 + x^3}{x^2}$

    d. $\dfrac{x^4 + x^3}{x - 1}$

    e. $\dfrac{x^5 + x^3}{x^2 - 1}$

54. A chest is filled with large gold and silver coins, weighing a total of thirty pounds. If each gold coin weighs 12 ounces, each silver coin weighs 8 ounces, and there are fifty coins in all, how many gold coins does the chest contain? (There are sixteen ounces in a pound.)

    a. 10

    b. 15

    c. 20

    d. 25

    e. 30

55. An ellipse is described by the equation $3x^2 + 4y^2 = 48$. What is the length of its major axis?

    a. $2\sqrt{3}$

    b. 4

    c. $4\sqrt{3}$

    d. 8

    e. 12

56. The first three terms of a geometric sequence are 80, 120, and 180. Which of the following is equal to the tenth term of the sequence?

    a. $\dfrac{5 \times 3^9}{2^5}$

    b. $\dfrac{5 \times 3^{10}}{2^7}$

    c. $\dfrac{5 \times 2^4}{3^{10}}$

    d. $\dfrac{5 \times 2^{13}}{3^9}$

    e. $\dfrac{5 \times 2^{14}}{3^{10}}$

57. If $f(x) = e^{x-3}$, $g(x) = 2x - 1$, and $h(x) = f(x) + g(x)$, then $h(3) =$

    a. 2

    b. 3

    c. 4

    d. 5

    e. 6

58. If $2 \sec \theta - \tan^2 \theta$, which of the following is a possible value for $\sec \theta$?

  a. 2
  b. $\sqrt{2}$
  c. $\sqrt{2} - 1$
  d. $2 - \sqrt{2}$
  e. $1 + \sqrt{2}$

59. The population of the town of Wrassleton has tripled every ten years since 1950. If P_0 is the town's population in 1950 and t is the number of years since 1950, which of the following describes the town's growth during this time?

  a. $P(t) = 10\, P_0^{3t}$

  b. $P(t) = P_0^{\frac{3}{10}t}$

  c. $P(t) = P_0 \times 3^{\frac{t}{10}}$

  d. $P(t) = P_0 \times \left(\frac{3}{10}\right)^t$

  e. $P(t) = \left(\frac{3}{10} P_0\right)^t$

60. If $f(1) = 2$, $g(2) = 3$, $f^{-1}(3) = 4$, and $g^{-1}(4) = 1$, which of the following is *not* necessarily true?

  a. $f\big(g(1)\big) = 3$
  b. $f\big(g(3)\big) = 1$
  c. $g\big(f^{-1}(2)\big) = 4$
  d. $g^{-1}\big(f^{-1}(3)\big) = 1$
  e. $g(2) = f(4)$

Answer Explanations #2

Reading

1. B: The two men are talking about four possible dimensions and their ability to move through them.

2. C: "Occasional" is very similar in meaning to "spasmodic."

3. C: It builds suspense because the Time Traveller already knows about the outcome of his experiments with time travel, and he is only leading his audience along by explaining the thought process behind it.

4. A: The characters in the selection are not given names, but occupation titles. The Time Traveller and the Medical Man are discussing their ideas here to give the reader a quick insight into their characters.

5. B: Lincoln begins this speech by discussing the founding of our country and what the original purpose of the U.S. was. Then, he goes on to talk about how the U.S. is currently engaged in a war intended to fracture the nation, and he states that the battle being discussed was one large tragedy that came out of the war. Next, Lincoln says that his speech and even the memorial itself can't truly honor those who died, and that it's up to those who survived to continue the fight to ensure the nation does not break apart. Answer B best communicates this message.

6. A: The ideas of the revolution are addressed in the first paragraph: Four score and seven years ago our fathers brought forth, upon this continent, a new nation, conceived in Liberty, and dedicated to the proposition that all men are created equal. This introduces the point that Lincoln is trying to make about the battle at hand and the war as a whole: the Civil War is threatening the ideas upon which the nation was created.

7. D: In the Gettysburg Address, Lincoln opens his speech with the phrase "Four score and seven years ago..." which is another way to say 87 years ago. After the opening paragraph with references to the past, Lincoln moves into observations on the present and appeals for action in the present. Dr. King's speech uses illustrations of his hope for the future of a diverse and peaceful America.

8. D: In the speech, King discussed important issues of race and equality while expressing his hope for the future.

9. C: People in government knew that the purchase would make the country more powerful, but the last sentence specifically states that they needed to explore. Answer choice C is the best prediction of what would occur next. Answer choices A and D infer too much, since you cannot assume any of these based on this passage given. Answer choice B is simply a statement that does not predict anything for the future.

10. C: Charles Dickens used a series of opposites to convey the idea that the period described involved conflicts between extremes of positive and negative, matched so equally that neither could win. He also introduced the tension of such conflicts around which the novel revolves—of love vs. hate and family vs. oppression. He was not ascribing all the contrasts to personal subjectivity (a), saying in comparing the past and present that they could not be separated (b), or attributing the extremes to the imagination of its most vocal experts (d).

11. D: Answer choice (D) correctly notes that Marcel's response overlooks important details within Adelaide's argument (i.e., the detail about the airborne chemicals and the detail about the natural products being effective) and as a result fails to offer a worthwhile objection. Answer choice (D) is correct.

12. B: According to the debate so far, rising hospital costs and insurance problems are good reasons to get the government involved in health care. However, the government will then control a big part of your life and can deny certain treatments. It seems like there are many pros and cons here: we must decide what we want to give up: some of our access to health care or some of our liberties.

This choice puts together all of the ideas from the speakers and summarizes them. It then illustrates important parts of the argument and draws a conclusion. Choices A and C only provide one side of the argument. Choice D summarizes but does not draw any conclusions.

13. A: The excerpt is written in first-person narration, meaning that the narrator is a character in the story, telling the story as he ("I") sees it. The narrator is not, however, omniscient, as there are many things about the situation that he does not know.

14. A: The correct answer is A, informational, because the author includes many factual details about the Nicaragua and Panama Canals. Choice B is incorrect because the author strictly gives facts and does not include jokes that would make the passage humorous. Choice C is incorrect because the author doesn't withhold details that would add mystery to the passive. Choice D is incorrect because the author does not show emotions such as anger; he has an objective tone.

15. C: The passage does not claim that studying a foreign language is essential to high school graduation (choice A). Choices B and D represent claims made in the passage, but do not include all of the claims made.

16. C: Clue words such as "as a child" and "later," as well as the use of dates, indicates that this passage is arranged in chronological order.

17. C: Here, the author is speaking of money management on a personal or household level.

18. B: This answer comes directly from the text and the narrator's elaborate description of his father's grave and its location. Options A and D describe things that the passage does not describe as vividly, while option C makes reference to a mirror reflection that is not mentioned in the passage at all.

19. C: Indigenous means originating or occurring naturally in an area or environment. This answer choice makes the most sense in the sentence context. The reason is that the birds were not native and were brought from Europe.

20. C: This is a rare case when both forms of *effect* (verb and noun) are used correctly in the sentence. The word *effect* is used as a verb when it expresses a specific desire to cause something to occur: *effect* a compromise, *effect* a change. The noun form of *effect* is the result of the change, so both forms are correct in this sentence. The form *affect* is incorrect in both places in the sentence.

Writing

1. B: is the correct answer because the verb should be in past tense rather than present tense. Choice A is incorrect because a comma should not separate the subject and verb of a sentence. Choice C is incorrect because it is better to write out *first* than it is to use numerical digits. Choice D

is incorrect because a comma is required to separate the dependent clause at the beginning of the sentence from the independent clause at the end of the sentence.

2. B: The other answer choices show a relationship between American pilots not having work because they gave up flying airplanes. The original sentences intend the opposite. Some American pilots returned from World War I without work in flying planes. So, they had to give up flying altogether and find other jobs.

3. B: is correct because a comma is needed to offset the non-essential clause *Roscoe Turner*. Choice A is incorrect because *Roscoe Turner* is a non-essential clause; it is not required to understand the meaning of the sentence. The clause should be offset by commas on both sides. Choice C is incorrect because *as* would change the meaning of the sentence to imply that Roscoe Turner dressed as a lion cub. Choice D is incorrect because the words *plane* and *airplane* can be used interchangeably.

4. C: is correct because the passage is discussing the past. Therefore, the past tense *could* is preferable over the present tense *can*. Choice A is incorrect because the comma is needed to set off the phrase at the beginning of the sentence. Choice B is incorrect because *traveled* only has a single *l*. Although both *a* and *its* could be used in this sentence, choice D is incorrect because *it's* is a conjunction for *it is* and would be incorrect if used in this part of the sentence.

5. B: is the best choice because it correctly transitions from the sentence 15 to sentence 16 and maintains the original meaning of the author.

6. D: is the best choice because it corrects the capitalization error in sentence 3. A, B, and C are not the best choices because they create new errors in sentence 3 instead of correcting the existing error.

7. B: is the best choice because sentence 5 functions as the thesis statement for this composition. A, C, and D are not the best choices because sentences 2, 3, and 1 do not function as the thesis statement for this composition.

8. C: is the best choice because sentence 10 is a comma splice with two independent clauses, and a semicolon is the best punctuation to correct this error. A is not the best choice because sentence 10 is a comma splice and must be corrected. B and D are not the best choices because they do not properly correct the sentence.

9. D: is the best choice because it accurately explains how sentence 21 functions as a transition between paragraphs 4 and 5. A is not the best choice because sentence 21 does function as a transition. B and C are not the best choices because they do not accurately explain how sentence 21 functions as a transition.

10. B: is the best choice because "appeared" is the most appropriate word to replace the misused word "appointed." A, C, and D are not the best choices because it would be inappropriate to replace the misused word with "approximated," "appropriated," or "appositioned."

11. A: is the correct answer because *its* without an apostrophe is the possessive form of the word *it*. *It's* with an apostrophe is a contraction for *it is*. Choice B is incorrect because *who* is used when the writer is referring to a subject rather than an object (*whom* is used for an object). Since *who* is referring to *students*, which could be a subject, *who* is the correct answer. Choice C is incorrect because *their* is the possessive form of *they*, while *they're* is a contraction for *they are*. Choice D is incorrect because it is correct to place a comma before a conjunction that precedes an independent clause.

- 71 -

12. D: is the correct answer because *furthermore* shows that Jeanette is presenting an additional point to support her argument. Choice A is incorrect because Jeanette is not presenting her final conclusion in this paragraph. Choice B is incorrect because the paragraph does not present a contrasting point; it has additional proof. Choice C is incorrect because *for that reason* is synonymous with *therefore,* which is also incorrect.

13. C: because it is grammatically correct and preserves the meaning of the original sentence. Choice A is incorrect because the second sentence combines a dependent clause with an independent clause preceded by a conjunction; this construction is not correct. Choice B is incorrect because the second sentence uses *because* when it should use *but.* Choice D is incorrect because the phrase *I didn't get enough feedback* does not support the preceding clause.

14. A: is the correct answer because *loose* is the opposite of tight while *lose* means to misplace something. Choice B is incorrect because *driver's* is possessive; the license belongs to the driver, which means the word needs an apostrophe. *Choice C* is incorrect because clauses separated by the word *because* should not be separated with a comma. Choice D is incorrect because a series of two items that is connected by *and* does not need a comma.

15. A: because the construction of dependent clause followed by independent clause best conveys the ideas of the lawmakers and the possible solution. Choice B is incorrect because it incorrectly uses a semicolon, which should only be used to separate two independent clauses. Choice C is incorrect because the first clause is missing the *if* that adds meaning to the sentence. Choice D is incorrect because the sentence construction is not parallel; *pass* and *creating* should be in the same verb form.

16. A: because a comma should follow a state name when it is used in this format. When a state name follows a city name, it becomes a non-essential clause and should be set off by commas. Choice B is incorrect because *it's* is a contraction for *it is* while *its* (without the apostrophe) is the possessive form of the word *it.* Choice C is incorrect because *buildings and places* is a two-item series connected by *and*; a comma should not be used in a two-item series written in this format. Choice D is incorrect for the same reason; the phrase is a two-item series connected by *and.*

17. B: is the correct answer because *Back in 1634* is a non-essential clause beginning the sentence and should be separated from the rest of the sentence by a comma. Choice A is incorrect because years should be written using Arabic numerals; they should not be written out. Choice C is incorrect for the opposite reason; in an essay, ordinals should be written out rather than using Arabic numerals. Choice D is incorrect because *unusually* changes the meaning of the sentence. Using the word *usually* helps indicate that the Boston Common was most often used for livestock but also had other uses.

18. B: While this information may appeal to some readers and certainly is evidence for Paul Revere being regarded as famous, this additional information will not maintain the focus of the passage. So, the author should not include this information.

19. D: because this choice most effectively explains how the New State House got its name. Choice A is incorrect because the word order of the sentence makes it difficult to understand why the New State House got its name; the dependent clause is not adequately supported. Choice B is incorrect because it changes the meaning of the sentence; the new building got its name from the old, not the other way around. Choice C is incorrect because it is in the passive voice and wordier from the correct answer.

20. D: because this version of the sentence is the most succinct and clear. Choice A is incorrect because the sentence is in the passive voice. Choice B is incorrect because it is not as clearly worded as choice D. Choice B separates the list of people from the reason why they are important (they are some of the most famous people in the cemetery), which makes the sentence difficult to understand. Choice C is incorrect because it is missing a comma after *Massacre* and because the sentence doesn't qualify how famous the people are. Only choice D explains that the people listed are the most famous people buried at the Granary.

21. D: This informal statement from the author shifts from the formal tone that has been established and is necessary for the addressed reader.

22. B: because the verb *could* means that something might happen; the word *potentially* means the same thing and is redundant. Choice A is incorrect because removing *soft* makes it unclear what type of drinks Elyse is referring to. Choice C is incorrect because the word *us* is required to know whom Elyse is talking about. Choice D is incorrect because the word *not* adds crucial meaning to the sentence; without the word, the reader would think Elyse was talking about drinking soft drinks in the high school.

23. B: because this sentence explains the benefits of the education that Elyse proposes. Choices A, C, and D are incorrect because they don't relate to the education plan that Elyse is proposing. These sentences might work better in the introductory or concluding paragraphs.

24. D: because a colon is used to set off a list. The phrase *including those chocolate chip cookies* is a non-essential phrase that should be separated from the sentence in some way, such as parentheses. Choice A is incorrect because the comma is required to separate the dependent clause from the independent clause. Choice B is incorrect because using the word *high* changes the meaning of the sentence; Elyse is not proposing that the prices for should be high; instead, she is proposing that certain items should cost more (or have higher prices) than others. Choice C is incorrect because *nutritional* is an adjective while *nutrition* is a noun.

25. A: because sentence 18 supports Elyse's previous point with an additional point. The word *furthermore* correctly connects these two points. Choices B and C are incorrect because these transition words are used for contrasting points, but Elyse is presenting two points that support each other. Choice D is incorrect because Elyse is not done with her argument at this point.

Mathematics

Arithmetic

1. A: One way to add or subtract mixed numbers is to first convert them to improper fractions. We can do this by multiplying the integer part of the mixed number by the denominator and adding that product to the numerator; this sum is the numerator of the improper fraction, and its denominator is the same as the denominator in the fractional part of the mixed number. So $4\frac{1}{5} = \frac{4\times5+1}{5} = \frac{21}{5}$ and $2\frac{1}{3} = \frac{2\times3+1}{3} = \frac{7}{3}$. Convert each fraction so that they contain the lowest common denominator, which in this case is 15. $\frac{21}{5} = \frac{21\times3}{5\times3} = \frac{63}{15}$ and $\frac{7}{3} = \frac{7\times5}{3\times5} = \frac{35}{15}$. We can now subtract: $\frac{63}{15} - \frac{35}{15} = \frac{28}{15}$. Finally, we convert back to a mixed number by dividing the numerator by the denominator. The quotient is the integer part, and the remainder is the new numerator; the denominator remains the same. $28 \div 15 = 1$ with a remainder of 13, so $\frac{28}{15} = 1\frac{13}{15}$.

2. B: To multiply numbers in scientific notation, first multiply the significands (the part before the power of ten), then multiply the powers of ten; when multiplying two numbers with the same base, add the exponents and keeping that base. So, to multiply 2.2×10^3 and 3.5×10^{-2}, we first multiply 2.2 by 3.5. To multiply decimals, first multiply the numbers normally ignoring the decimal point; then, position the decimal point in the answer so that the number of digits after the decimal point in the product is equal to the *sum* of the number of digits after the decimal point in both factors. $22 \times 35 = 770$, and since there is one digit after the decimal point in 2.2 and one digit after the decimal point in 3.5, there should be two digits after the decimal point in the product, which therefore becomes 7.70, or 7.7. Now, multiply the powers of 10: $10^3 \times 10^{-2} = 10^{3+(-2)} = 10^1$. The final answer is 7.7×10^1.

3. C: Recalling that percent just means "divided by 100," each of the given numbers can be represented as fractions:

I. $\dfrac{58}{67}$

II. $0.58 = \dfrac{.58}{100} = \dfrac{58}{10,000}$

III. $58\% = \dfrac{58}{100}$

IV. $5.8\% = \dfrac{5.8}{100} = \dfrac{58}{1,000}$

All of the fractions share the same numerator. Among fractions with the same numerator, the largest fraction has the smallest denominator. We can order these fractions from greatest to least by ordering the denominators from least to greatest. The correct order is $\dfrac{58}{67} > \dfrac{58}{100} > \dfrac{58}{1,000} > \dfrac{58}{10,000}$ which corresponds to choice C.

4. A: Together, these three angles form a straight angle, or 180°. So, $x + y + z = 180°$, which means $z = 180° - x - y = 180° - 91° - 42° = 47°$.

5. B: If he has covered $\dfrac{1}{2}$ the distance after two hours, and $\dfrac{2}{3}$ the distance after four hours, and he does not backtrack, then the fraction of the distance he has covered after three hours must be between $\dfrac{1}{2}$ and $\dfrac{2}{3}$. To compare fractions, we can convert them to equivalent fractions with the least common denominator. The least common denominator of $\dfrac{2}{3}$ and $\dfrac{3}{4}$ is 12; $\dfrac{2}{3} = \dfrac{2 \times 4}{3 \times 4} = \dfrac{8}{12}$ and $\dfrac{3}{4} = \dfrac{3 \times 3}{4 \times 3} = \dfrac{9}{12}$. Since $\dfrac{9}{12} > \dfrac{8}{12}$, $\dfrac{3}{4}$ is not between $\dfrac{1}{2}$ and $\dfrac{2}{3}$. The least common denominator of $\dfrac{1}{2}$ and $\dfrac{2}{5}$ is 10; $\dfrac{1}{2} = \dfrac{1 \times 5}{2 \times 5} = \dfrac{5}{10}$ and $\dfrac{2}{5} = \dfrac{2 \times 2}{5 \times 2} = \dfrac{4}{10}$. Since $\dfrac{4}{10} < \dfrac{5}{10}$, $\dfrac{2}{5}$ is not between $\dfrac{1}{2}$ and $\dfrac{2}{3}$. Similarly, $\dfrac{4}{5} = \dfrac{4 \times 4}{5 \times 4} = \dfrac{16}{20}$ and $\dfrac{3}{4} = \dfrac{3 \times 5}{4 \times 5} = \dfrac{15}{20}$; since $\dfrac{16}{20} > \dfrac{15}{20}$, $\dfrac{2}{5}$ is not between $\dfrac{1}{2}$ and $\dfrac{2}{3}$. However, $\dfrac{3}{5} = \dfrac{3 \times 2}{5 \times 2} = \dfrac{6}{10} = \dfrac{3 \times 4}{5 \times 4} = \dfrac{12}{20}$; $\dfrac{6}{10} > \dfrac{5}{10}$ and $\dfrac{12}{20} < \dfrac{15}{20}$, so $\dfrac{1}{2} < \dfrac{3}{5} < \dfrac{3}{4}$.

6. A: x percent is the same thing as $\dfrac{x}{100}$, and finding x percent of a number is the same as multiplying that number by x percent. This is true even when the number is itself a percent. So, 10% of 40% is $40\% \times 10\% = 40\% \times \dfrac{10}{100} = 40\% \times \dfrac{1}{10} = 4\%$.

7. D: To multiply decimals, first multiply the numbers normally ignoring the decimal point; then, position the decimal point in the answer so that the number of digits after the decimal point in the product is equal to the *sum* of the number of digits after the decimal point in both factors. $262 \times 71 = 18,602$; there are two digits after the decimal point in 2.62 and one digit after the

- 74 -

decimal point in 7.1, so there should be three digits after the decimal point in the product, which is therefore 18.602.

8. C: The ratio of volumes on two objects of the same shape is equal to the *cube* of the ratio of their lengths. Therefore, if the ratio of the length of the large cube to that of a building block is $\frac{20 \text{ cm}}{4 \text{ cm}} = 5$, the ratio of the *volume* of the large cube to that of a building block is 5^3, or 125— so that is how many building blocks it will take to make the large cube.

9. C: When comparing fractions it is necessary to find common denominators.

A. $\frac{1}{2} = \frac{6}{12} > \frac{1}{3} = \frac{4}{12} > \frac{1}{4} = \frac{3}{12}$

B. $\frac{1}{5} = \frac{4}{20} < \frac{3}{10} = \frac{6}{20} < \frac{7}{20}$

C. $\frac{7}{9} = \frac{49}{63} > \frac{2}{3} = \frac{42}{63} > \frac{6}{7} = \frac{54}{63}$ <Correct>

D. $\frac{1}{5} = \frac{70}{350} < \frac{2}{7} = \frac{100}{350} < \frac{3}{10} = \frac{105}{350}$

Once all of the fractions have been represented using common denominators, it is easy to determine which line of inequalities is not valid. Among the four choices, the only invalid inequality is choice C.

10. C: 149 is close to 150, and 1502 is close to 1500. Therefore, we would expect $\frac{149}{1502}$ to be close to $\frac{150}{1500}$, which reduces to $\frac{1}{10}$. As a decimal, $\frac{1}{10} = 0.1$. Choice C is the closest to this number.

11. C: We can start by rewriting the rate of drainage in gallons per minute. $\frac{1 \text{ gallon}}{15 \text{ seconds}} \times \frac{60 \text{ seconds}}{1 \text{ minute}} = \frac{60 \text{ gallons}}{15 \text{ minutes}} = 4$ gallons/minute. This means that in t minutes, the tub will have drained $4t$ gallons. We are asked to find how long the tub will take to drain 12 gallons, so $4t = 12$; dividing both sides by 4, we find $t = 3$.

12. B: While we *could* multiply together all the numbers in the numerator and all the numbers in the denominator and then simplify, it would be easier to cancel what we can first. There is a factor of 7 in both the numerator and the denominator; we can cancel those. The same goes for a factor of 3. That leaves us with $\frac{1}{8} \times \frac{2}{1} \times \frac{4}{5} \times \frac{1}{1}$. We can go further, though; since $2 \times 4 = 8$, the 2 and the 4 in the numerator cancel the 8 in the denominator, leaving us with just $\frac{1}{1} \times \frac{1}{1} \times \frac{1}{5} \times \frac{1}{1}$, or simply $\frac{1}{5}$.

13. C: To find the average, add together all the numbers and then divide by how many there are (in this case three). In order to add decimal numbers, write them one above the other with the decimal points aligned and carry out the addition normally, placing the decimal point in the same position in the result:

2.02

+ 0.275

+ 1.98

4.275

Now, to divide, just carry out the division normally but put the decimal point in the same position in the quotient as ti appears in the dividend:

$$
\begin{array}{r}
1.425 \\
3\overline{)4.275} \\
\underline{3} \\
1\ 2 \\
\underline{1\ 2} \\
07 \\
\underline{6} \\
15 \\
\underline{15} \\
0
\end{array}
$$

14. B: The three constants given are gamma, phi, and pi, respectively. The sum of the three is greater than 5. The next three choices are each raised to the gamma power. Gamma is equal to about ½. Because all three are raised to the same power and because all three are positive, we know that the one with the smallest base is the smallest number. The difference of pi and phi is less than phi so choice B is the least of those three. Because choices B, C, and D all have positive bases less than 5 raised to a power less than 1, all three must be less than 5. Hence, choice B is the smallest number.

15. A: When dealing with percents or fractions, "of" generally means multiply; 60% of $\frac{5}{6}$ means 60% $\times \frac{5}{6}$. We can write $x\%$ as $\frac{x}{100}$; 60% is therefore $\frac{60}{100}$, which reduces to $\frac{6}{10} = \frac{3 \times 2}{5 \times 2} = \frac{3}{5}$. So 60% of $\frac{5}{6} = \frac{3}{5} \times \frac{5}{6} = \frac{3 \times 5}{5 \times 6} = \frac{3}{6} = \frac{1}{2}$.

16. D: One foot is equal to twelve inches, so the road is twelve inches long on the map. If the map's scale is 1 inch = 5 miles, then we can find the road's actual length by solving the proportion $\frac{12 \text{ inches}}{x \text{ miles}} = \frac{1 \text{ inch}}{5 \text{ miles}}$, or simply $\frac{12}{x} = \frac{1}{5}$. One way to solve this is by cross-multiplying: $12 \times 5 = x \times 1$, so $x = 60$.

17. C: We can do this by multiplying the integer part of the mixed number by the denominator and adding that product to the numerator; this sum is the numerator of the improper fraction, and its denominator is the same as the denominator in the fractional part of the mixed number. So, $3\frac{1}{4} = \frac{3 \times 4 + 1}{4} = \frac{13}{4}$ and $2\frac{5}{6} = \frac{2 \times 6 + 5}{6} = \frac{17}{6}$. Convert each fraction to its equivalent so that both fractions contain the lowest common denominator, which in this case is 12. $\frac{13}{4} = \frac{13 \times 3}{4 \times 3} = \frac{39}{12}$ and $\frac{17}{6} = \frac{17 \times 2}{6 \times 2} = \frac{34}{12}$. We can now add: $\frac{39}{12} + \frac{34}{12} = \frac{73}{12}$. Finally, we convert back to a mixed number by dividing the numerator by the denominator. The quotient is the integer part, and the remainder is the new numerator; the denominator remains the same. $73 \div 12 = 6$ with a remainder of 1, so $\frac{73}{12} = 6\frac{1}{12}$.

18. D: Taking a percent of a number means multiplying by that percent: if 50 is $P\%$ of 40, then $50 = 40 \times P\%$. That means $P\%$ is just $\frac{50}{40}$. We can write that as a decimal by dividing, putting a decimal point after the dividend and adding zeroes as necessary:

$$
\begin{array}{r}
1.25 \\
40\overline{)50.00} \\
\underline{40} \\
10\,0 \\
\underline{8\,0} \\
2\,00 \\
\underline{2\,00} \\
0
\end{array}
$$

So $\frac{50}{40} = 1.25$. To convert to a percent, we can multiply by 100, which is equivalent to moving the decimal point two places to the right: $1.25 = 125\%$.

19. A: When comparing decimals, compare them one decimal place at a time. First compare the part before the decimal point; whichever has the largest whole part is largest. If the whole parts are equal, compare the tenths place, the place just after the decimal point; if they differ in that place, then whichever has the larger digit in that place is larger. If the digits in the tenths place are the same, compare the hundredths place, the second place after the decimal point, and so on. In this case, all the decimals have a zero before the decimal point, so we'll start by comparing the tenths place. 0.55, 0.500, and 0.505 all have a 5 in the tenths place, while 0.0555 has a zero in the tenths place. So, 0.55, 0.500, and 0.505 are larger than 0.0555. Now, compare the hundredths place of the remaining choices, discarding the 0.0555 that we now know is smallest. 0.55 has a 5 in the hundredths place, while 0.500 and 0.505 both have zeroes. So, 0.55 is the largest of the choices.

20. B: To convert a number to scientific notation, move the decimal point until there is just one digit before it (not counting leading zeroes), and rewrite the number as the result times a power of ten. The exponent of the power of ten is equal to the number of places the decimal point was moved— positive if the decimal was moved left, and negative if the decimal was moved right. Starting with 0.05, to put only one digit before the decimal point, we have to move the decimal point two places to the left. Therefore, $0.05 = 5 \times 10^{-2}$, and choices A and C are equal. To convert a percent to a decimal, divide it by 100, which is equivalent to moving the decimal point two places to the left: so $5\% = 0.05$, and choices A and D are equal. However, expressed as a fraction, $0.05 = \frac{5}{100} = \frac{5 \times 1}{5 \times 20} = \frac{1}{20} \neq \frac{1}{50}$. So choices A, C, and D are equal, but B is not equal to the other three.

Quantitative Reasoning, Algebra, and Statistics

21. D: To solve this problem, all we need to do is substitute -1 for every x in the expression and then simplify: $\frac{2(-1)-2}{(-1)+3} = \frac{-2-2}{2} = \frac{-4}{2} = -2$.

22. C: The expected value is equal to the product of the theoretical probability of getting a 4 after one roll, and the number of rolls, 10. Thus, the expected value is $\frac{1}{6} \cdot 10$, or $\frac{5}{3}$.

23. B: To simplify the inequality $x^2 + 2x \geq x + 6$, we can first move all the terms to the left-hand side: $x^2 + 2x - x - 6 \geq 0$, which, after combining like terms, becomes $x^2 + x - 6 \geq 0$. We can now factor the left-hand side; since the leading coefficient is 1, one way to do this is to look for two numbers that add to the coefficient of x (here 1) and multiply to the constant term (here -6). The two numbers that qualify are -2 and 3, so $x^2 + x - 6 = (x - 2)(x + 3)$. This makes the inequality $(x - 2)(x + 3) \geq 0$. We know the dividing points for the regions that do and do not satisfy the inequality are then at $x - 2 = 0$ and at $x + 3 = 0$, that is at $x = 2$ and at $x = -3$. Consider the sign in each region: when $x < -3$, then $x - 2$ and $x + 3$ are both negative, and their product is positive. When $-3 < x < 2$, then $x - 2$ is negative and $x + 3$ is positive, so their product is negative. When $x > 2$, then then $x - 2$ and $x + 3$ are both positive, and their product is again positive.

$(x - 2)(x + 3) \geq 0$ when $x \leq -3$ or $x \geq 2$. This is correctly represented by choice B.

24. C: Probably the simplest way to solve this equation is to first get rid of the fractions by multiplying each term by their lowest common denominator, which is $6x$: then we have

$\frac{6x}{2x} + \frac{6x}{x} = \frac{6x}{6}$, which reduces to $3 + 6 = x$. So, $x = 3 + 6 = 9$.

25. B. The median of a data set is the middle element of the set after it is sorted in numerical order. In this example the median is 2.

26. B: If there are n floors, and each floor has a height of h feet, then to find the total height of the floors, we just multiply the number of floors by the height of each floor: nh. To find the total height of the building, we must also add the height of the spire, 30 feet. So, the building's total height in feet is $nh + 30$.

27. B: First, let's distribute the x and y that are outside the parentheses and then combine like terms: $(y - 2) + y(3 - x) = (xy - 2x) + (3y - xy) = -2x + 3y + xy - xy = -2x + 3y$.

28. D: Any negative number is less than any positive number, so $-\frac{1}{4}$ must be the first in the list. For numbers with equal numerators, the number with the greater denominator is smaller. So $\frac{1}{5} < \frac{1}{3}$, and $\frac{1}{3} < \frac{1}{1} = 1$. The correct ordering for the given numbers is, therefore, $-\frac{1}{4}, \frac{1}{5}, \frac{1}{3}, 1$.

29. A: The average number of male students in the 11th and 12th grades is 125 $\left(\text{calculated as } \frac{131 + 119}{2}\right)$. The number of Hispanic students at the school is 10% of 1219, which is 122 students (rounded up from 121.9). The difference in the number of male and female students at the school is $630 - 589 = 41$, and the difference in the number of 9th and 12th grade students at the school is $354 - 255 = 99$.

30. C: Since the triangle is covering part of the square, the total area of the figure is the area of the triangle plus the area of the square that is not covered. The area of the triangle is calculated as $A = \frac{1}{2}bh$. The base is equal to the side length of the square, s, and the height is given to be $3s$. Thus the area of the triangle is $\frac{3s^2}{2}$. The area of the square not covered by the triangle is a pair of smaller triangles, each with a height of s. While we are not given enough information to find the exact base of either of these triangles individually, we can determine that the sum of their bases is $\frac{s}{3}$. This means that the total exposed area of the square is $\frac{1}{2} \times \frac{s}{3} \times s = \frac{s^2}{6}$. The total area of the figure then is $\frac{3s^2}{2} + \frac{s^2}{6} = \frac{9s^2 + s^2}{6} = \frac{10}{6}s^2 = \frac{5}{3}s^2$.

31. D: A basic definition for probability is success over total. In this case, the total is football players and the success is band members who also play football. The ratio 0.35/0.42 is equal to about 83%.

32. D: Use the rule that $(a + b)(a - b) = a^2 - b^2$ or multiply the binomials using the FOIL method: multiply together the First term of each factor, then the Outer, then the Inner, then the Last, and add the products together.

$$(x + 6)(x - 6) = x \times x + x \times (-6) + 6 \times x + 6 \times (-6) = x^2 - 6x + 6x - 36 = x^2 - 36.$$

33. B: First, determine the proportion of students in the fifth grade. Since the total number of students is 180, this proportion is $\frac{36}{180} = 0.2$, or 20%. Next, determine the same proportion of the total prizes, which is 20% of 20, or $0.2(20) = 4$.

34. D: There are several ways to solve a system of equations like this. One is by substitution. If $x + 2y = 3$, then $x = -2y + 3$. Substituting that into the other equation, $-x - 3y = 4$, we get $-(-2y + 3) - 3y = 4 \Rightarrow 2y - 3 - 3y = 4 \Rightarrow -y - 3 = 4 \Rightarrow -y = 7 \Rightarrow y = -7$. Now, putting that value for y back into one of the original equations, we get $x + 2(-7) = 3 \Rightarrow x - 14 = 3 \Rightarrow x = 17$.

35. C: Since 3 of the 15 songs are by Beyonce, the probability that any one song will be by Beyonce is $\frac{3}{15} = \frac{1}{5}$. The probability that the next song is NOT by Beyonce is $\frac{4}{5}$. Therefore the probability that the next two songs are both not by Beyonce is $\frac{4}{5} * \frac{4}{5} = \frac{16}{25}$.

36. B: The average is the total amount spent divided by the number of students. The first three students spend an average of $10, so the total amount they spend is $3 \times \$10 = \$30$. The other six students spend an average of $4, so the total amount they spend is $6 \times \$4 = \$24$. The total amount spent by all nine students is $\$30 + \$24 = \$54$, and the average amount they spend is $\$54 \div 9 = \$6$.

37. C: We can find the probability we need by adding the distinct probabilities that a student attends Elm OR likes comedies. However, we must also remember to subtract off the probabilities that a student attends Elm AND likes comedies. Our previous calculation double counted these students. The probability may be written as $P(\text{Elm or Comedy}) = \frac{750}{1650} + \frac{675}{1650} - \frac{350}{1650}$, which simplifies to $P(A \text{ or } B) = \frac{1075}{1650}$ or approximately 65%.

38. B: $-\frac{3}{2}\left(\frac{1}{2} + \frac{1}{3}\right) - \frac{2}{3}\left(\frac{1}{2} - \frac{3}{4}\right) = -\frac{3}{2}\left(\frac{3}{6} + \frac{2}{6}\right) - \frac{2}{3}\left(\frac{2}{4} - \frac{3}{4}\right) = -\frac{3}{2}\left(\frac{5}{6}\right) - \frac{2}{3}\left(-\frac{1}{4}\right) = -\frac{3 \times 5}{2 \times 6} + \frac{2 \times 1}{3 \times 4} = -\frac{15}{12} + \frac{2}{12} = -\frac{13}{12}$. Finally, to convert this to a mixed number, divide the numerator by the denominator; the quotient is the integer part, and the remainder is the new numerator, while the denominator remains the same. $13 \div 12 = 1$ with a remainder of 1, so $-\frac{13}{12} = -1\frac{1}{12}$.

39. C: Neither Texas' maximum nor the fact that New Mexico has had more volunteers on 10 occasions is indicative of the number of volunteers that should be expected in the future. In fact, Texas has a smaller mean and median than New Mexico and similar spreads. Mean is most closely related to expected value and closely related to median in symmetric distributions. Choice C is the best answer.

40. C: To solve an equation with an absolute value like $|x^2 - 2| = x$, we can treat it as two separate cases. If $x^2 - 2$ is positive, $|x^2 - 2| = x^2 - 2$, and the equation becomes simply $x^2 - 2 = x$, which can be rewritten as the quadratic equation $x^2 - x - 2 = 0$. Since the leading coefficient is 1, we can factor this quadratic equation by finding two numbers that add to the coefficient of x (–1) and

- 79 -

multiply to the constant term (−2); the two qualifying numbers are 1 and −2, and the equation factors to $(x + 1)(x − 2) = 0$, yielding the solutions $x = −1$ and $x = 2$. If $x^2 − 2$ is negative, then $|x^2 − 2| = −(x^2 − 2)$, and the equation becomes $−(x^2 − 2) = x$, which we can rewrite as $x^2 + x − 2 = 0$. Again, this can be factored, as $(x − 1)(x + 2) = 0$, yielding the two additional solutions $x = 1$ and $x = −2$. However, this method of solving equations with an absolute value may result in spurious solutions, so we should check all these solutions in the original equation to make sure that they are genuine. A shortcut for this step is to see that x is equal to an absolute value, so it must be positive. You can then verify that 1 and 2 are both valid in the original equation, and determine that the equation has two valid solutions.

College Level Mathematics

41. E: To combine a number of exponential terms, it is generally a good start to convert them to equivalent terms containing the same base. In this case, since two of the terms already have a base of $\sqrt{2}$, it may be easiest to convert them all to that base, using the fact that when an exponential is raised to a power, the exponents are multiplied: $(a^b)^c = a^{bc}$. So, $2^{\sqrt{2}} = \left(\sqrt{2}^2\right)^{\sqrt{2}} = \sqrt{2}^{2\sqrt{2}}$. The equation then becomes $\sqrt{2}^2 \times \sqrt{2}^{2\sqrt{2}} = \left(\sqrt{2}^{\sqrt{2}}\right)^x$, the right-hand side of which simplifies to $\sqrt{2}^{\sqrt{2}x}$. As for the left-hand side, we can simplify it using the fact that when terms of the same base are multiplied, the exponents are added: $a^b \times a^c = a^{b+c}$. So $\sqrt{2}^2 \times \sqrt{2}^{2\sqrt{2}} = \sqrt{2}^{2+2\sqrt{2}}$, and we have $\sqrt{2}^{2+2\sqrt{2}} = \sqrt{2}^{\sqrt{2}x}$, which implies $2 + 2\sqrt{2} = \sqrt{2}x$. Dividing both sides of the equation by $\sqrt{2}$, we obtain $\sqrt{2} + 2 = x$.

42. E: One way to solve a system of inequalities is to plot both inequalities and see where they overlap. In this case, the first inequality describes the interior of a circle, and the second a half-plane; plotting them both on the same graph produces this:

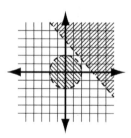

There is no overlap between the shaded areas representing the two inequalities. Therefore, this system of inequalities has no solution.

43. C: The change of base formula for logarithms states that $\log_a x = \frac{\log_b x}{\log_b a}$ for any positive base b. Since $\ln x$ is equivalent to $\log_e x$, we can apply to change of base formula to get $\frac{\ln 81}{\ln 3} = \log_3 81$. $\log_3 81$ can be written as $\log_3 81 = x$, which, by the definition of a logarithm, can be written in standard notation as $3^x = 81$. Since $81 = 3^4$, $\log_3 81 = 4$.

44. D: The quadratic expression $x^2 − 4x + 5$ is not easily factorable, so its roots are best found using the quadratic formula, $x = \frac{−b \pm \sqrt{b^2 − 4ac}}{2a}$. Putting in $a = 1$, $b = −4$, and $c = 5$, this yields $x = \frac{−(−4) \pm \sqrt{(−4)^2 − 4 \times 1 \times 5}}{2 \times 1} = \frac{4 \pm \sqrt{16 − 20}}{2} = \frac{4 \pm \sqrt{−4}}{2} = \frac{4 \pm 2i}{2} = 2 \pm i$.

45. A: This problem is most easily solved using the *law of sines*, which states that the ratio of the sine of each angle in a triangle to the length of the opposite side is equal: $\frac{\sin A}{a} = \frac{\sin B}{b} = \frac{\sin C}{c}$. In this case, angle θ is opposite side a, and the angle with a measure of $30°$ is opposite side b, so we can write $\frac{\sin \theta}{a} = \frac{\sin 30°}{b}$. Since $\sin 30° = \frac{1}{2}$, this becomes $\frac{\sin \theta}{a} = \frac{1/2}{b}$, or $\sin \theta = \frac{a}{2b}$.

46. D: If the two lines intersect at the point $(2, 3)$, that means $x = 2, y = 3$ is a solution to both equations, and we can substitute in those values for x and y to yield $3 = 2a + b$ and $3 = 2b + 2a$. We now have two equations and two unknowns. There are many ways to solve this system of equations, including the substitution method. We can solve the first equation for $2a$ and substitute the result into the second equation, which also contains the term $2a$: the first equation solved for $2a$ is $2a = 3 - b$, and when this value for $2a$ is substituted into the second equation, we can solve for b: $3 = 2b + (3 - b) \Rightarrow 3 = b + 3 \Rightarrow b = 0$. Since we already know $2a = 3 - b$, this means $2a = 3 - 0 = 3$, so $a = \frac{3}{2}$.

47. D: The difference between any two consecutive odd integers is 2. If there are three consecutive odd integers, therefore, and the middle number is x, the other two integers must be $x - 2$ and $x + 2$. So their product is $x(x - 2)(x + 2) = x(x^2 - 4)$ (since $(a - b)(a + b) = a^2 - b^2) = x^3 - 4x$.

48. C: Consider the end behavior of the function. If b were even, then the function would either go to ∞ on both ends or to $-\infty$ on both ends; either way, both ends of the function must be on the same side of the x-axis; therefore, if the function crosses the x-axis, it has to cross it again to get back to the same side as it started. In other words, for an even function, it is impossible for the function to cross the x-axis only once unless the function's maximum or minimum value touched the x-axis, and this scenario is eliminated in the problem. Therefore, b cannot be even, which means b must be odd. (a may be either positive or negative, and c may or may not be zero.)

49. B: Suppose you put the two hosts in two adjacent seats, as required. (It does not matter which two seats we choose since we are not worried about rotations of the whole arrangement.) Then, the other four guests can be arranged in $4! = 4 \times 3 \times 2 \times 1 = 24$ different orders. However, we have to multiply this answer by 2 because there are two possible ways in which the two hosts can be seated; in other words, if they are sitting side-by-side, the hosts can exchange seats and still be sitting together. The total number of orders is $24 \times 2 = 48$.

50. B: The equation $y = 2 \sin(\pi x - \pi)$ can be rewritten as $y = 2 \sin(\pi(x - 1))$. The general form of a sine function is $y = A \sin(B(x - C)) + D$, where the amplitude (the vertical distance from the peak to the center) is $|A|$, the phase shift (horizontal shift) is C, the vertical shift is D, and the period (the width of one full cycle) is $\frac{2\pi}{B}$. In this case, the amplitude is 2, the phase shift is 1, the vertical shift is 0, and the period is $\frac{2\pi}{\pi} = 2$. All of the graphs show the same (correct) amplitude and vertical shift; they only differ in their periods and phase shifts. Consider first the period. The width of one full cycle in the graph is 2 for choices A and B, and 4 for C, D, and E. Since the given function has a period of 2, this means the correct choice must be A or B. Choice A shows what the sine graph would look like without a phase shift: it starts at $x = 0$, then rises to a peak $\frac{1}{4}$ of the way through its period at $x = \frac{2}{4} = \frac{1}{2}$, then crosses the x-axis again halfway through its period at $x = \frac{2}{2} = 1$, and so on. However, the given function has a phase shift of 1, so the entire graph should be shifted right 1 unit. Choice B correctly shows this function.

51. A: If f^{-1} is the inverse of f, then by definition $f^{-1}(f(x)) = x$; therefore, $f\left(f^{-1}(f(x))\right) = f(x) = e^{2x}$.

52. C: The given equation is the standard equation for a plane in three dimensions. More specifically, if a, b, and c are all nonzero, it is a plane not parallel to any of the coordinate axes.

53. D: To simplify this rational expression, we can first factor out the largest common power of x on both sides of the fraction: $\frac{x^7+2x^6+x^5}{x^4-x^2} = \frac{x^5(x^2+2x+1)}{x^2(x^2-1)} = \frac{x^5}{x^2} \times \frac{x^2+2x+1}{x^2-1} = x^3 \times \frac{x^2+2x+1}{x^2-1}$. Now, we can factor both the numerator and denominator of the fraction. The numerator is a quadratic equation that can be factored using the quadratic formula or by other means, but the easiest way to factor it is to recognize it as the square of a binomial: $(a + b)^2 = a^2 + 2ab + b^2$, so $x^2 + 2x + 1 = x^2 + 2(x)(1) + 1^2 = (x + 1)^2$. Similarly, the denominator is a difference of squares: $(a + b)(a - b) = a^2 - b^2$, so $x^2 - 1 = x^2 - 1^2 = (x + 1)(x - 1)$. The expression becomes $x^3 \times \frac{(x+1)^2}{(x+1)(x-1)} = x^3 \times \frac{x+1}{x-1} = \frac{x^3(x+1)}{x-1} = \frac{x^4+x^3}{x-1}$.

54. C: We can write the problem as a system of two linear equations. Let x be the number of gold coins, and y be the number of silver coins. Since there are fifty coins total, we have $x + y = 50$ as one of the equations. If each gold coin weighs 12 ounces, then the total weight in ounces of the gold coins is $12x$; similarly, the total weight in ounces of the silver coins is $8y$. Since all the coins together weigh 30 pounds, which is equal to $30 \times 16 = 480$, we have $12x + 8y = 480$. Because each term in this equation is divisible by 4, we can divide the whole equation by 4 to get $3x + 2y = 120$; this is not a required step, but does make the numbers a little smaller and more manageable.

We now have two equations: $x + y = 50$ and $3x + 2y = 120$. There are a number of ways to solve a system of equations like this. One is to the substitution method. We can solve the first equation for y to get $y = 50 - x$, and then substitute this into the second equation to get $3x + 2(50 - x) = 120$. After distributing the 2, we get $3x + 100 - 2x = 120$; combining like terms gives $x + 100 = 120$, and, finally, subtracting 100 from both sides yields $x = 20$. Therefore, the number of gold coins is 20.

55. D: The standard form of the equation of an ellipse is $\frac{x^2}{a^2} + \frac{y^2}{b^2} = 1$, where a and b are the lengths of the semimajor and semiminor axes—that is, half the lengths of the major and minor axes. The major axis is the longer axis, while the minor axis is the shorter. To put the equation $3x^2 + 4y^2 = 48$ in standard form, we have to divide both sides of the equation by 48: $\frac{3x^2}{48} + \frac{4y^2}{48} = \frac{48}{48} \Rightarrow \frac{x^2}{16} + \frac{y^2}{12} = 1 \Rightarrow \frac{x^2}{4^2} + \frac{y^2}{\left(2\sqrt{3}\right)^2} = 1$. The lengths of the semimajor and semiminor axes are 4 and $2\sqrt{3}$, and the lengths of our major and minor axes are $2(4) = 8$ and $2\left(2\sqrt{3}\right) = 4\sqrt{3}$. Since $8 > 4\sqrt{3}$, the length of the major axis is 8.

56. A: A geometric sequence is a sequence in which the ratio between any two consecutive terms is the same; this ratio is called the *common factor*. The nth term of a geometric sequence with first term a_1 and common factor r is $a_1 r^{n-1}$. In this case, the first term is 80 and the common factor is $\frac{120}{80} = \frac{3}{2}$, so the tenth term is $80 \times \left(\frac{3}{2}\right)^{10-1} = \frac{80}{1} \times \left(\frac{3}{2}\right)^9 = \frac{80 \times 3^9}{2^9} = \frac{2^4 \times 5 \times 3^9}{2^4 \times 2^5} = \frac{5 \times 3^9}{2^5}$.

57. E: If $h(x) = f(x) + g(x)$, then $h(3) = f(3) + g(3)$. $f(3) = e^{3-3} = e^0 = 1$, and

$g(3) = 2 \times 3 - 1 = 6 - 1 = 5$, so $h(3) = 1 + 5 = 6$.

- 82 -

58. E: The simplest way to solve this problem is to first use the trigonometric identity

$\sec^2 \theta = \tan^2 \theta + 1$, or $\tan^2 \theta = \sec^2 \theta - 1$. Replacing $\tan^2 \theta$ with $\sec^2 \theta - 1$, the given equation becomes $2 \sec \theta = \sec^2 \theta - 1$. Moving everything to one side of the equation, we get $\sec^2 \theta - 2 \sec \theta - 1 = 0$. If we let $x = \sec \theta$, this is a simple quadratic equation, $x^2 - 2x - 1 = 0$. We can solve this using the quadratic formula, $x = \frac{-b \pm \sqrt{b^2 - 4ac}}{2a}$. In this case, $x = \frac{-(-2) \pm \sqrt{(-2)^2 - 4(1)(-1)}}{2(1)} = \frac{2 \pm \sqrt{4 - (-4)}}{2} = \frac{2 \pm \sqrt{8}}{2} = \frac{2 \pm 2\sqrt{2}}{2} = 1 \pm \sqrt{2}$. So, $\sec \theta = 1 \pm \sqrt{2}$.

59. C: If the town's population triples every ten years, this is an example of *exponential growth*, which is described by the equation $P = P_0 e^{kt}$, where P is the population at time t, P_0 is the initial population, and k is growth rate. To find k, we can use the fact that ten years after 1950 the town's population will be three times what it started with: i.e., when $t = 10$, $P = 3P_0$. So, $3P_0 = P_0 e^{10k}$; we can cancel out the P_0 from both sides to get $3 = e^{10k}$. Taking the natural logarithm of both sides, we get $\ln 3 = 10k$, so $k = \frac{1}{10} \ln 3$. So our exponential growth equation is $P(t) = P_0 e^{\left(\frac{1}{10} \ln 3\right)t} = P_0 e^{\ln 3 \left(\frac{t}{10}\right)}$; using the fact that $a^{bc} = \left(a^b\right)^c$, we can rewrite this as $P(t) = P_0 \left(e^{\ln 3}\right)^{\frac{t}{10}}$. But e^x and $\ln x$ are inverse functions, so $e^{\ln 3} = 3$, and this becomes $P(t) = P_0 \times 3^{\frac{t}{10}}$.

As an alternate way of solving the problem, we can just plug in $t = 10$ to each equation and see which one then yields the proper value of $P(10) = 3P_0$. Respectively, the five choices give $P(10) = 10 P_0^{30}, P_0^3, 3P_0, P_0 \times \left(\frac{3}{10}\right)^{10}$, and $\left(\frac{3}{10}P_0\right)^{10}$; only choice C yields the correct answer.

60. B: A property of inverse functions important for this problem is that if $f(x) = y$, then $f^{-1}(y) = x$. Therefore, from the given information that $f(1) = 2$, $g(2) = 3$, $f^{-1}(3) = 4$, and $g^{-1}(4) = 1$, it also follows that $f^{-1}(2) = 1$, $g^{-1}(3) = 2$, $f(4) = 3$, and $g(1) = 4$. So $f(g(1)) = f(4) = 3$, and choice A is true. $g(f^{-1}(2)) = g(1) = 4$, and choice C is true. $g^{-1}(f^{-1}(3)) = g^{-1}(4) = 1$, and choice D is true. $g(2) = 3 = f(4)$, and choice E is true. The only choice that does *not* follow from the given information is choice B; since we do not know the value of $g(3)$, we cannot determine the value of $f(g(3))$.

Thank You

We at Mometrix would like to extend our heartfelt thanks to you, our friend and patron, for allowing us to play a part in your journey. It is a privilege to serve people from all walks of life who are unified in their commitment to building the best future they can for themselves.

The preparation you devote to these important testing milestones may be the most valuable educational opportunity you have for making a real difference in your life. We encourage you to put your heart into it—that feeling of succeeding, overcoming, and yes, conquering will be well worth the hours you've invested.

We want to hear your story, your struggles and your successes, and if you see any opportunities for us to improve our materials so we can help others even more effectively in the future, please share that with us as well. **The team at Mometrix would be absolutely thrilled to hear from you!** So please, send us an email (support@mometrix.com) and let's stay in touch.

If you feel as though you need additional help, please check out the other resources we offer:

Study Guide: http://mometrixstudyguides.com/ACCUPLACER

Flashcards: http://mometrixflashcards.com/ACCUPLACER